BEADS
in bloom

The art of making French beaded flowers

A **BEADWORK** HOW-TO-BOOK

ARLENE BAKER

INTERWEAVE PRESS

Editor: Jean Campbell
Illustration: Gayle Ford
Photography, except as noted: Joe Coca
Cover and interior design: Bren Frisch
Production: Dean Howes
Copy editor: Stephen Beal
Proofreader: Nancy Arndt

Beadwork® magazine
Interweave Press
201 East Fourth Street
Loveland, Colorado 80537-5655 USA
www.interweave.com

Printed in Asia by Tien Wah Press

Library of Congress Cataloging-in-Publication Data

Baker, Arlene, 1944-
    Beads in bloom: the art of making French beaded flowers / Arlene Baker.
        p. cm.
    ISBN 1-931499-06-3.
        1. Bead flowers. I. Title.

TT890.2 .B35 2002
745.58'2—dc21   2001059209

First printing: IWP-10M:1201:TWP

Enough for me
At times to see
A flower an angel ought to wear.

—*Walter Savage Landor*

Acknowledgements

To my students who share my enthusiasm and inspire me. Without them, there is no reason to write this book.

And to my husband David for his devotion and encouragement. Without him, there is no book.

My warmest thanks to:

Jean Campbell, my editor, for providing a once-in-a-lifetime opportunity.

The staff at Interweave Press for their efforts on behalf of this book.

Kathy Gastellu, my longtime friend, for providing the computer link and being the messenger.

Gaillen Smith, first a student and now a friend, for taking time to read the pages and offer suggestions and encouragement.

Marie Delight, my dear Mom, for being there when I need her. I'm so glad she can share this with me.

Herb Delight, for providing support and executing my designs in wood. I'm glad you're part of the family.

Candace Kling, for sharing her experiences and words of wisdom.

Jonalee Crabb, for generously allowing me to use her research.

Joanne Verde, for saving me at the last minute by returning two beaded flowers she purchased from me.

All the beadwork artists who eagerly loaned their vintage flowers and their own handiwork for the photos in this book.

Contents

Introduction and History

WHO MADE THE FIRST BEADED FLOWERS? What inspired them? When were the flowers made? These seemed like important questions that deserved to be answered in a book about the art of making beaded wire flowers.

I thought the answers to these questions would be easy to find but, in fact, they weren't. In my quest, I discovered that very little is known about the true origins of this craft, that documentation is limited, and that the stories that exist are vague and often contradictory. For example, no one seems to know why the technique is called "French" beading.

What knowledge has filtered down through the years may be merely gossip (someone recently told me that Napoleon once said that "history is a set of lies agreed upon"), but because the following information has been repeated frequently, I'm considering at least these elements to be true.

The craft dates to the Middle Ages and was introduced in Venice where bead production was a widely practiced trade by highly skilled craftsmen. The sheer abundance of wondrous glass beads in this area contributed to the development of beaded flowers.

Women of modest means, who sold or traded the flowers for their livelihood, fashioned them with beads and wire. The elaborate decorative arrangements that they made adorned altars, banquet tables, and statuary during most religious festivities and other celebrations.

By the mid-nineteenth century, the craft had become very popular in France. Although some might find this fact grim, the flowers were commonly used to ornament gravesites and tombs.

In the Victorian era, when women had more leisure time and a vast interest in nature, they took up the craft. They used the flowers to beautify their homes as well as for personal adornment.

The popularity of beaded flowers continued through the 1920s and 1930s; there is even evidence to support the contention that prisoners off the coast of Brittany were required to make the flowers in great numbers to support the demands of the market.

If your curiosity about these lovely flowers is just minimally satisfied by these answers, then think of this as a rare opportunity to use poetic license and imagine your own story. For example, in her book about the early twentieth-century art of making flowers with ribbons, my good friend Candace Kling writes, "In the past, without modern refrigeration and transportation, many months went by without the sight of fresh flowers in the house. We take for granted, and cannot imagine how exotic and expensive it was to have flowers out of season. To fill this void, women surrounded themselves with objects adorned with blooms of all kinds, carved,

Early 1900s box. From the collection of the author.

painted, and stitched in a myriad of forms. Ribbon-work afforded them the luxury of flowers in winter." It's easy to imagine that these women also created beaded flowers for the very same reasons.

As to the reason for the craft's resurgence in the 1960s and 1970s when most books about how to make French beaded flowers were written, one can only speculate about the answer. Perhaps it had to do with that time in our turbulent past when many artistic people thought that flower-power ruled.

Throughout history, beadwork has been "in" or "out" and has had its ups and downs of popularity along with fashion. But to me the reasons don't really matter. And the history, whether fact or fiction, is not nearly as important as the satisfaction derived from making the beaded flowers.

For the past several years, it's been my pleasure to share my vintage beaded flower collection with enthusiastic students and all who express an interest in this newly popular craft. Together we marvel at the skills and creativity of these unknown artisans as we strive to recreate their methods to make the same glorious flowers.

I am delighted to have this opportunity to share with you these breathtaking pieces and the techniques I have learned from them. It is my hope that you will use this book to fashion a beautiful beaded flower that will one day inspire someone from another era to become interested all over again in the art of French beaded flower making.

Arlene

Beading Tools and Supplies

UNLIKE MANY HANDICRAFTS, beaded flower making requires few tools and supplies. In the beginning you can get by with just the basics.

Beads
Wire
Needle-nose pliers
Cutters
Scissors
Cotton and silk floss, nylon cord
Transparent tape
Glue
Ruler

Later when you have gained experience and learned how to use the basics, you'll want to invest in some additional tools to make beading easier.

Nylon jaw wire straighteners
Wire spool holders
Round-nose pliers
Heavy-duty snapper cutters
Awl

For large flower arrangements, you'll want to add planting materials such as floral or molding clay; sand, pebbles, or moss; and a variety of vases, pots, baskets, and other containers. And for jewelry making, you'll need an assortment of findings that include pin clasps, earring backs, pierced surface jewelry discs, and filigree stampings in assorted sizes.

Beads

A round or almost round object with a hole in it, a profusion of twinkling stars in a dramatic darkened sky; something you can put on a string, or glinting pinpoints of light that sparkle like the dewdrops on a gossamer web—no matter your initial reaction to the subject of beads, you'll find the perpetual beauty of a spectacular beaded flower impossible to resist.

Beads can be bought in hundreds of colors and a variety of materials, shapes, and sizes. They are readily available in bead stores, craft and hobby shops, mail-order catalogs and magazines, and over the Internet.

Only glass beads are used for making beaded flowers. They are sold in tubes, boxes, and bags, and on stringed bunches called hanks. There are transparent, translucent, lined, dyed, and opaque beads that are round, cut or faceted beads that are more irregular, and bugle beads that are short or long and narrow.

The best size and shape for most flowers is a size 11° round seed bead. Smaller sized seed beads (12°, 13°, and 14°) make delicate miniatures and slender stamens. Larger sized 10°s, cut or faceted beads, and bugle beads of various lengths are pleasing accents in specialized flower designs. Seed beads in sizes 8°, 6°, and occasionally 4° are used for finishing flower stems. They can also be used to striking effect as the center Basic of larger petals and leaves.

Buy beads you love, but be sure to include some you may not at first be attracted to. They could turn out to be just the right ones to add an unexpected touch of vibrant color to a flower. You'll be happy to have beads in a rainbow of colors and all the shades in between. You may not always know their purpose when you buy them, but they'll inspire you and help you make choices. Even though beads strung on threads are easier to put on spool wire, don't resist those perfect loose beads just because they're not strung.

Let nature be a teacher. Look at flower books and gardening magazines. Experiment and be creative—it's okay to break rules. Trust your instincts. Color choice is personal, so if you want a beaded blue rose, make it and enjoy.

Wires

Beading Wire

There are many brands of beading wire on the market today suitable for making beaded flowers.

You can find beading wire in bead stores, craft and hobby shops, and hardware stores. It usually comes on spools in a variety of sizes designated by gauges and in many colors beyond the traditional imitation silver and gold.

Since any wire you use will change the color of your beads, your choice of brands and colors is a matter of experimentation and personal preference. The best way to find your favorite is to purchase an assortment of this relatively inexpensive wire and learn what works best for you and your projects.

The wire sizes used most often are 28, 26, and 34 gauge. The higher the number, the thinner the wire. The thinner the wire, the more flexible it is. You will use 28-gauge wire for petals and leaves that need to bend and curve and twist with minimum support. You will use 26-gauge wire for petals and leaves that need firm support. You'll use 34-gauge wire for lacing, for binding on petals and leaves, and for assembly. It can also be used for tiny, delicate flower petals and greenery.

It's important to know that gold (brass) and colored wires are softer and therefore more flexible than silver-colored wire of the same gauge. If you are just beginning to learn beaded flower making, you may find it difficult to master the techniques and achieve the best results using these softer wires. The wire I use and recommend most often is the least expensive silver-colored wire.

Stem Support Wires

When flower stems need to be reinforced or lengthened, it is often preferable to use something stronger than the spooled beading wire. A heavier gauge wire suitable for this purpose can be found in most craft or hobby shops, hardware stores, or stores that specialize in florist supplies.

Unlike the beading wire available on spools, this wire is usually sold packaged in 18" straight-cut lengths that are perfect for the stems of beaded flowers. It comes in faux silver and several painted colors and a variety of sizes designated by gauge. Do not be concerned with the appearance or color of the wire because it will always be hidden by a covering of beads, embroidery floss, or cording on the finished stem. The most popular sizes of packaged wire are 18, 20, and 22 gauge. It's a good idea to have on hand an assortment of sizes so you have a choice whenever you need to reinforce or lengthen a stem.

Stem Coverings

Embroidery Floss and Nylon Cord

Embroidery floss is an inexpensive way to give the stems of your beaded flowers a look of old-fashioned elegance similar to those silk wrapped beauties found in lavish vintage bouquets. The floss comes in a vast array of wonderful colors, it's readily available almost everywhere, and it's very easy to use. Nylon cording is another superb thread to consider when you want to try an alternative to wrapping stems with embroidery floss.

A type of jewelry twine like Conso® #18 Bonded Nylon Thread has a completely different texture from the floss and is more luminous. The color selection is somewhat limited, but the cord is inexpensive and may be purchased in most bead stores, from mail-order catalogs, and through magazines that specialize in jewelry supplies.

Try your hand with both materials and you'll be amazed at your ability to immediately create finely finished flowers.

Silk Floss

The most luxurious thread you can use to finish the stems of your beaded flowers is 100 percent silk.

Silk covers the stem wires beautifully and is simple to apply. If you've been hesitant to work with silk floss because of cost or a limited choice of colors, now is the right time to try it. There is a new stranded six-ply silk currently on the market called Eterna Silk® Stranded. It comes in five-yard skeins and is readily available in an artist's palette of colors from your local yarn and needlecraft stores or by mail order. Best of all, the price is very affordable. When you use this or any similar silk product, you won't see any difference between the stems of those silk-wrapped vintage blooms you admire and your own beaded flowers. So go ahead and spoil yourself; there's no longer a good reason to avoid the sensuous pleasure of working with real silk thread.

Floral Tape

Floral tape is another type of material you can use for a stem covering. It's a narrow (½" wide) crepe paper that comes on a roll. The tape becomes tacky on both sides when stretched. This product was the one most often used for stem finishes during the 1960s and 1970s when beaded flower making was experiencing an extended period of popularity. Because the tape covers the stems quickly, it remains a favorite of some beaded flower makers today. For me, it has certain limitations. Color choice is extremely narrow, over time the tape discolors badly, and it can leave a sticky residue on the beads. Unless you're very meticulous when you apply it, it makes the stems too bulky.

Even though floral tape is not my choice for a stem covering, you should try it at least once. It's an inexpensive item that may be purchased from most craft or floral supply shops. Use it, then make your own decision whether or not you like this finish on the stems of your beaded flowers.

Findings

Findings are the metal parts that can transform your beaded flowers and greenery into exquisite jewelry.

For example, make a single rose and pin it on your blouse or jacket lapel. Use a row of tiny forget-me-nots or pansies to adorn a necklace or barrette. Make a pair of daisies, attach them to some earrings, and you have the perfect accessory for a summer day.

Most findings can be purchased from bead stores and craft shops. You can also order findings by mail.

These products (pin clasps, stick pins, necklace clasps, ear clips, etc.) are readily available in both expensive and inexpensive materials. The difference between them, both in quality and workmanship, is easy to see. Don't chance spoiling the overall look of your beaded flower jewelry by using the least expensive findings. Always buy the best ones you can afford for your project.

Search for pin clasps with narrow bars that fit behind the flower stem. Take time to choose a necklace clasp that complements the beads. Use perforated disks (pierced surface metal that resembles a showerhead) or ornamental filigree stampings to hide bare wires the way professional jewelry makers do.

Your jewelry will be set off by these better findings and your efforts to create something special will be apparent to everyone who sees your finished work.

A Potpourri of Helpful Hints and Good Things to Know

Tools

Always buy the best tools you can afford. There really is a difference between tools that just get the job done and quality tools that make the job easier, less frustrating, and more pleasurable as well.

If you take classes, it's a good idea to mark your tools in some manner (engrave or write your name, or tie a ribbon on the handle) so you can identify them easily. Most beadworkers use the same tools and unintentional mix-ups occasionally do happen.

Work Area and Work Habits

Some artists can bead anywhere, while others need a workroom or a studio. Some beadworkers keep everything neat; those more like me have bits and pieces scattered all over. Where and how you choose to bead is a matter of personal preference, but there are a few very important considerations that affect everyone who loves the art.

You must have adequate lighting, a comfortable chair, and a table or lap tray you can position at the correct height. It helps to have a simple storage system to keep your beads and tools organized. Use plastic bags or small jars and containers with lids to hold your beads. A tackle box or toolbox with compartments will store your tools.

Beading can be relaxing, but you will put stress on your body if you stay in the same position for long periods of time. Take frequent breaks, move around, and stretch your neck to ease muscle tension. Be sure to rest your eyes.

Tips Worth Trying

Old fashioned aluminum hair clips ("clippies") are the extra pair of hands you need in your bead work. Use them to support rows of beads when you're working very large petals or leaves. (Clip one across the top of the unit and one across the bottom. As you work the rows, open one clip, slip the beaded wire under, close the clip, and continue working.) Use them to hold beaded rows as you lace them together or to keep larger flower parts in position before you join them to make the flower. Hair clips in various lengths are easy to find in drugstores, supermarkets, and beauty supply shops.

Tiny plastic clothespins (1¼" length) are another useful item when you need more than ten fingers or because you feel like you're all thumbs. A few of the clothespins' many uses include holding a pin clasp in place before you secure it to the stem, keeping beads on stem wires until you assemble the flower, and securing thread ends while glue is drying.

Wire straighteners (Eurotool®) have nylon jaws and look like a pair of pliers. You can straighten and smooth bent wire (all gauges) by pulling it between the tool's closed jaws. The nylon jaws don't mar or damage the wire, so there's less chance of breakage later. Once you own a pair of wire straighteners, you'll wonder how you made French beaded flowers without them.

A wire spool holder is a reusable device that holds an opened spool of beading wire. Designed out of necessity as an aid for my students, it will keep bare wire or beaded wire from spiraling off the spool, out of control. To use it, simply take the top (or the bottom; it unscrews from either end) off the holder, put your spool of wire on the dowel, and replace the top. Holders come in several sizes to accommodate all types of spooled beading wire and sets are available from me.

There are many glues on the market. When you are working with floss and cording, choose a glue that is water soluble and dries clear (Aleene's Tacky Glue® is one I highly recommend). For gluing findings to bare wire, use E6000® or a similar jeweler's cement.

Shaping each flower component is an important part of the finishing process. It can make the difference between a realistic piece and a lifeless copy. It's a good idea to have on hand an assortment of rounded and pointed objects (tweezers, toothpicks, dowels of all sizes, slim pencils or pens, manicure sticks, etc.) to use for shaping.

A bead spinner is a handy gadget that can speed up the bead stringing process. A bead spinner is a tool that knitters and crocheters use to string beads, but it can also be used for this purpose. It works best when you use a heavy-gauge spool wire. To use the spinner, bend the end of the spool wire to resemble the needle that comes with the spinner. Pour your beads (they must be loose) into the wooden bowl and turn the spinner. If it works (and sometimes it doesn't), the beads will jump onto the spool wire. When enough beads are strung, simply cut off the bent end of the wire. Make a wire knot to keep the beads from sliding off the end.

Tricks of the Trade

Most of the illustrations in this book make the work appear very loose with wide spaces between the wire and the beads. This is necessary to define processes. In real life, all wire twists, wraps, and beading should be tight and close together.

Beads that are too big, too thin, or just oddly shaped need to be removed from the spool wire. Remove them by grasping the misshapen bead between the tips of your needle-nose pliers, cupping one hand over the tool, turning your face away, and crushing the misshapen bead. Do this carefully so you don't damage or accidentally cut the wire.

When you're making flowers, try to keep the beads close together to prevent bare wire from showing between them. Once in a while this is unavoidable. When too much wire shows between the beads in some places, make it less conspicuous by dabbing a little craft paint that matches the bead color on the bare wire. Use a fine artist's brush and take care to avoid painting the beads.

Train yourself to twist and wrap the wire consistently in one direction. Keep the spool wire STRAIGHT at all times. This is especially important when you are using the Basic Technique. To make these kinds of petals and leaves look as pretty as possible, hold the Top Basic Wire in one hand and the Bottom Basic Loop in the other hand and pull them in opposite directions. Do this frequently as you work and especially at the end when the last row of the unit is completed but before the petal or leaf is finished.

Even though you do your best to avoid kinks, from time to time you will get them in the spool wire. These kinks are susceptible to breaking, so it is important to remove them promptly. As soon as you see a bend in the wire, stop beading. Don't pull the wire. Don't use your pliers. Push your fingernail into the bend and force it open. Hold the wire close to the bend and swing the part you are holding around in one direction and then the other until the bend is almost gone. Use your wire straighteners or your fingers to smooth the wire further and continue with the beading. If the wire breaks (and it does happen), sometimes you can add a new piece of wire to the broken end (inconspicuously twisting both ends together), but more often than not it's better to start the beading over.

When you're using different size beads to make one flower, keep the flower parts in proportion.

Always keep finished flower parts separated from the beads and beaded spool wire until you are ready to assemble the flower. Put the parts in plastic resealable bags, envelopes, or other small containers to avoid a hopelessly tangled mess. If you are working on more than one flower, make labels to identify the pieces, "leaves for daisy," "petals for rose," and so on. The labels will keep the parts organized and easy to find when you need them.

Fundamental Techniques

ALL FRENCH BEADED FLOWERS are made with beads that are held in place with wire. The wire is shaped into petals and leaves ("units") using two main techniques, the Loop and the Basic. These two techniques, used alone, or in combination with one another, are the foundation for all other design variations and give each flower its own distinctive form and appearance.

Twists and Wraps

Wire twists and wire wraps are the two methods used to hold the beads in place.

A Loop of beads may be secured with a twist (as in Single Loops) or a twist and a wrap (as in Wrap-around Loops).

When the Basic Technique is used, the beads are always locked in place with twists and wraps. The instructions will tell you when to use each method.

It is important to understand the difference between a twist and a wrap and how to do them. When two wires are used to make a twist, both wires are locked together and cannot be loosened unless they are twisted in the opposite direction. When two wires are used to make a wrap, one wire remains straight and the other wire is curved around it. The straight wire can be pulled loose from the wrapping wire. A wrap is not as secure as a twist, so use the wrap method only when directed.

The key to making perfect twists and wraps is to control the wire with proper hand positions and movements. There are several ways to hold the wire. Because of how the various flower parts are constructed, you will want to learn all of them to achieve the best results.

Wire wrap

Wire twist

Beading the Wire

Open the spool of wire the same way you open a spool of sewing thread. The wire will spiral around the spool if you've loosened the correct end.

Unwind about twelve inches of wire. Cut the end of the wire at an angle to make a sharp point, trimming away any part that was bent or crimped by the spool. If you have a set of wire spool holders, now is the time to use one. If not, put the spool in a small plastic resealable bag to keep the wire from becoming unruly.

Pull the length of wire you unwound through the middle of a folded paper towel or soft cloth several times to clean it if it feels gritty or looks discolored. Straighten the wire.

There are many ways to string beads on the wire.

You can pour loose beads into a plastic container or shallow bowl, dipping and scooping the end of the wire through the beads and catching several on the wire each time. Or you can pour a small number of beads in the palm of your hand and pick them up one at a time with the end of the wire held in your other hand. A third way is to spill a small number of beads on a suede cloth, moisten the end of your finger, press your finger into the beads, and use the end of the wire to pick them off your finger one at a time. Repeat until the required measurement of beads is strung. You can use the pattern directions to calculate the amount you need or string at least 20" to get you started.

If you are working with a hank of beads, first wrap a piece of tape around the loose thread ends just above the knot at the top of the beads. The tape will keep the hank from coming apart and insure that no beads are lost as the strands are removed one by one. Gently remove one end of one strand from the hank. If the strand doesn't pull out easily, cut the thread close to the knot. Hold this end of the beaded strand between the thumb and forefinger of one hand and use your other hand to insert the end of the wire through as many beads as possible, usually about one inch. Pull out the thread from these beads and let them slide back toward the spool (Figure 1).

Here's another way. Carefully remove the entire

Figure 1

strand from the hank and tape one end to your work surface. Pull the strand taut with one hand and use your other hand to insert the end of the wire through the beads, allowing them to slide on the wire as you remove the thread. Continue transferring beads until you have strung one or two strands on the wire. Any misshapen beads or beads that do not go on the wire easily should be discarded. If you use only a portion of a strand, the end of the thread may be tied around the last bead or you can fold a small piece of tape over the thread just below the last bead. Either method will keep beads from sliding off the strand. After all the beads have been strung, knot the wire.

To make a wire knot, form a single loop (without beads) close to the end of the wire. Turn the loop clockwise two or three times to twist the wires together, then bend the short end of the wire up toward the loop so you don't stick your finger on it later (Figure 2).

Do not cut the beaded wire from the spool until

Figure 2

you have completed the petal or leaf you are making. Unless otherwise instructed, or you run out of beads before completing the unit, all work is done with the beaded wire attached to the spool.

Should you run out of beads before completing the unit, you must estimate the length of wire needed to finish. For Loops, measure the length of the Loop and multiply it by the number of Loops remaining plus about five or six inches; for the Basic Technique, go around the petal or leaf with the bare wire for the required number of remaining rows plus about five or six inches. Once you've made your estimation, cut that length of wire from the spool and add the extra beads.

Be sure to knot the wire after you string the beads, then finish the petal or leaf.

Bead Count and Measurement

New students eagerly want to know, "How do I make a French beaded flower?" If you're asking yourself the same question, you make the flowers by counting and measuring the beads.

While there are many other parts in the process (stringing the beads on the spool wire, choosing a pattern and technique, assembling the flower, finishing, and so on), measuring and counting the beads plays the most important role.

Measuring determines the size of the pieces that form the flowers, offers a way to work accurately, and helps you estimate the amount of beads you'll need on the spool wire.

At first this method sounds impossible, and like everyone your initial reaction may be dismay. But, wait. It's not nearly as tedious as it sounds; with practice the work goes fast, and it really is a simple way to guarantee the symmetry of each lovely flower that you fashion.

For example, a particular pattern may direct you to make petals for a flower as in "make three, Continuous Single Loops, five on one wire, 1" of beads per Loop." This means you must make three separate and complete Continuous Single Loop units and

that each unit will have five 1" Loops on a single wire.

To calculate how many inches of beads to string for each unit, multiply the number of Loops times the number of inches per Loop. In this case, 5 × 1" = 5" of beads per unit. To determine the total for three units, multiply 5" × 3 and you know to string at least 15" of beads on the spool wire. (It's a good idea to add an extra inch or two in case you need to remove some irregular shaped beads during construction.)

To make one unit, measure 1" of beads each time before you make a Loop or count the number of beads in 1" and use the bead count instead. Either way the results are the same, so choose the method that is easiest for you.

When the instructions tell you the number of beads, as in "make five, Continuous Single Loops, six on one wire, with 10 beads to each Loop, there is no decision to make. No need to measure, just count the beads.

If you are using the Basic Technique, the pattern may say "make four leaves, Basic 1½", Rows 3, Pointed Top, Round Bottom." This means you must make four separate and complete pieces. Each one will have a Pointed Top and a Round Bottom; a Basic Count that measures 1½" and a total of 3 Rows of beads. You will measure the beads for the Basic Count and count the number of rows as you make them (it's not necessary to count the beads in the rows). The Basic Count is always Row 1.

You can use the Basic Count measurement (1½") times the number of Rows (3) to estimate how many inches of beads to string on the spool wire for each leaf unit (1½" × 3 = 4½"). Always allow one or two inches extra since the number of beads increases slightly with each row.

To estimate the total for the four separate units, multiply 4½" × 4 and you know you need to string at least 18" of beads on the spool wire.

When the instructions tell you the number of beads to use for the Basic Count as in "make four leaves, Basic 7, Rows 3, etc.," simply count the 7 beads and the number of rows as you make them. No measuring is required.

These examples are meant to be a guideline. Please take the time to read the complete instructions for the Fundamental Techniques (Loop and Basic) before you begin to make your beaded flowers.

Stem Wires

All completed petals, leaves, and other flower parts have wire extensions below the beads. These wires are used for the stems. When the beaded components are made with Loops, each unit will have two extensions, the knotted end of the wire at the beginning (Wire A) and the bare spool wire (Wire B) at the end (Figure 3).

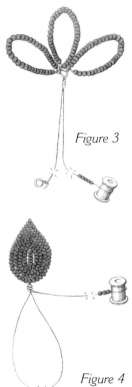

Figure 3

If the Basic Technique is used to construct a unit, it's possible for each unit to have three wire extensions—the Bottom Basic Loop cut in two and a length of bare wire cut from the spool (Wire B) (Figure 4).

Plan to leave all wire extensions long. If you're generous with this measurement, the extensions will usually be the only wire you'll need for the stem when you assemble the flower.

Figure 4

Important Items to Remember as You Begin

⚜ Keep the wire under control, but handle it gently as you make your wraps and twists.

⚜ Don't worry (overwork) the wire; it can break and will at the worst possible place. Repairs are difficult, so a good rule to follow is, if the wrap or twist isn't perfect, start over or leave it alone.

⚜ Be generous with the wire; you can always trim the length. But if it's too short, it's usually too late.

⚜ Always knot the spool wire whenever you finish beading it and immediately after cutting it. This will be easy to remember once you forget and your beads scatter and you have to pick them up and restring them.

⚜ Straighten the wire frequently.

⚜ Clean your hands often; natural oils and perspiration will hinder your ability to grip the wire.

⚜ Practice really does make perfect. You may feel clumsy, awkward, and all thumbs at first; but beading gets easier and you will be rewarded if you don't give up.

Loops

Many flowers and much greenery can be made entirely with Loops. There are Single Loops, Twisted Loops, Wraparound Loops, and Crossover Loops. These Loops can stand alone or you can make Continuous Loops in a series, traveling horizontally or laterally along one length of wire.

The design variations may be used by themselves, or combined within a single flower. For example, the delicate blue flowers in the vintage bouquet in the photo below are each made with three continuous single loops and one four-row crossover for the center. Look closely at the photo at right

and you will see that one complete Loop unit (five Continuous Single Loops on one wire) by itself is a charming flower when the flowers are grouped in quantity.

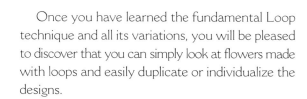

Once you have learned the fundamental Loop technique and all its variations, you will be pleased to discover that you can simply look at flowers made with loops and easily duplicate or individualize the designs.

Single Loops

Slide the required number of beads to within 4"–6" of the knotted end of the wire. This is a good working length for most flowers. You may increase this measurement depending upon the desired finished length of the stem (See Stem Wires, page 18). This bare wire section will be referred to as Wire A. The beaded feed wire still attached to the spool will be referred to as Wire B and the work in progress is in the middle.

Hold these beads in place and slide the remaining strung beads back toward the spool to expose a 3"–4" length of bare spool Wire B. This exposed wire is working wire and will give you room to make the Loop. With the work in front of you, keep Wire A horizontal and extended to the left, and Wire B (the bare portion only) horizontal and extended to the right. Now make a loop of the counted beads by crossing Wire B over Wire A directly below and close to the beads (think of writing a lowercase script letter "e"). See Figure 1.

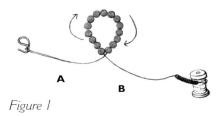

Figure 1

Be sure the beads on the loop are tight. Hold them in place where the wires cross with the thumb and forefinger of one hand while you turn the Loop clockwise one time with the other hand. This action will twist the two wires together and secure the beaded Loop. That's all there is to it (Figure 2).

Figure 2

The Single Loop may be left rounded or you can narrow it by gently pinching the sides together (Figure 3).

If one Single Loop is all you need to complete the unit, it's a good idea to turn the Loop one or two times more while you're still holding it. This action will prevent the twist from loosening when the flower is assembled later (Figure 4).

Figure 3

Figure 4

To finish the unit, slide the remaining strung beads back toward the spool to expose a length of bare spool Wire B equal to the length of Wire A. Cut the wire from the spool at this measurement. Be sure to knot the spool Wire B so the strung beads do not slide off. Pull both wires down below the Loop and straighten them. Trim both ends evenly, cutting away the wire knot (Figure 5).

Twisted Loops

Make a Single Loop with the number of beads required for your pattern. Narrow the Loop by pinching the sides together. Support the Loop by placing the base (where the wires are twisted) between the thumb and forefinger of one hand and grasp the top of the Loop with your other hand. Gently turn the Loop in one direction so that the sides of the Loop twist

Figure 5

together. Take care to avoid twisting too tightly or the beads may chip or break. The length of the Loop and the design of the flower will determine the number of twists (Figure 6). Finish the Twisted Loop as previously instructed for the Single Loop.

Figure 6

Figure Eight Loop

To make this variation of a Twisted Loop, begin as before with a Single Loop and narrow it. Then, instead of supporting the base of the Loop, move the thumb and forefinger of one hand to the middle of the Loop. Gently turn the top of the Loop one time with your other hand. Leave the Figure Eight Loop narrowed or open the circles by carefully inserting an awl or round toothpick above and below the twist (Figure 7). Finish the Figure Eight Loop as you did the Single Loop.

Figure 7

Wraparound Loops

A Wraparound Loop is made by wrapping an extra row or multiple rows of beads around a Single Loop. The first Single Loop is not included in the wraparound count. If the instructions direct you to wrap once, the finished Wraparound Loop will have two rows of beads—the Single Loop and one row wrapped around it. If you are told to wrap twice, the finished Wraparound will have three rows of beads, and so on.

Depending on the size of the beads and the way the petal is used in the finished piece, Wraps of four or more rows may require lacing to support them (see Lacing, page 54). To make your petal or leaf sturdier, you will need to use your own judgment whether to lace multiple row Wraparound Loops or switch to the Basic Technique.

To make a Wraparound Loop, begin with a Single

Vintage miniature pansies made with round, horizontal, and oval Wraparound Loops grouped with greenery and flowers made with the Basic Technique. Collection of the author.

Loop with the number of beads required for your pattern (Figure 8). (See Single Loops, page 19.)

Figure 8

To make the Wraparound row, slide beads from the beaded spool Wire B toward the base of the Loop you just completed. Bring the beaded wire up and wrap it all the way around the Loop (traveling counterclockwise). No count or measurement is necessary—just be sure the beads fill the Wrap completely as you go around the outside of the Single Loop with the beaded wire (Figure 9).

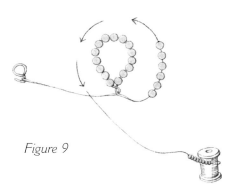

Figure 9

Keep the Wrap close to the Single Loop and the beads tight. Stop where you began at the base of the Loop, with Wire B in front, crossed over Wire A directly below the beads. Hold the beads in the Wrap

in place with one hand and use your other hand to slide the extra beads back toward the spool to expose a length of bare Wire B. Swing Wire A down below the loop and straighten it (Figure 10). This

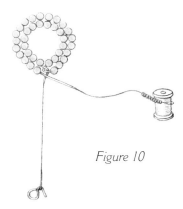

Figure 10

action will enable you to wrap Wire B around Wire A in the same manner in which you wrap around a Top Basic Wire, (see Basic Technique page 34).

Use the thumb and forefinger of one hand to hold the Loop where Wire B is crossed over Wire A. Use your other hand to bring Wire B counterclockwise around the back of the Loop and across the front again. Keep the beads in place and pull the wire so it wraps tightly around Wire A directly below the beads (Figure 11).

Use your thumbnail to push Wire B close to the base of the Loop. To make additional wraps around the unit, keep Wire A straight below the beads and repeat the process.

To secure the final wraparound row and finish one unit, wrap bare Wire B around Wire A two more times directly below the beads before releasing the Loop. Wrap Wire B side by side, not over itself, to avoid bulky wires at the base of the Loop.

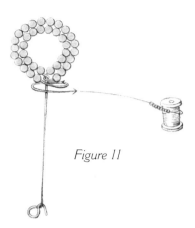

Figure 11

Figure 13

Follow the shape of the flattened Loop as you proceed with the wraparound rows.

It's also possible to make an Oval Wraparound in the same manner if you begin with a Single Loop that has been shaped into an oval.

Crossover Loops

A Crossover Loop is actually two Single Loops of beads that cross each other at the top. When the Crossover Loop has beading up the front and bare wire down the back, it is called a Three-Row Crossover. When the Crossover Loop has beading up the front and beading down the back, it is called a Four-Row Crossover. These Loops may be pressed flat or left dimensional. I think the Crossover Loop looks best when the initial Single Loop has an even number of beads because you need to divide them in two.

To begin, make a Single Loop with the number of beads required for your pattern. If the bead count is an odd number (13, 15, 17, etc.) subtract or add one bead to make the bead count even (12, 14, 16, 18, etc.). Gently press both sides together to expose a small section of bare wire and create a space between the beads at the top of the loop. The Crossover Loop will be anchored in this space later. Make sure there is an equal number of beads on either side of the bare wire (Figure 14).

Release the Loop. Leave Wire A below the Loop. Slide any remaining strung beads back toward the spool to expose a length of bare Wire B equal to the length of Wire A. Cut wire from the spool at this measurement. Be sure to knot the end of Wire B so the beads do not slide off. Pull Wire B down below the Wraparound Loop, next to Wire A. Straighten the wires and trim both ends evenly, cutting away the wire knot (Figure 12).

Figure 12

The shape of the single loop determines the shape of the subsequent wraparound rows. To make a Horizontal Wraparound Loop, first make a Single Loop with the number of beads required for your pattern. Support the base of the Loop with one hand and use your other hand to press down on the top of the Loop until it narrows horizontally (Figure 13).

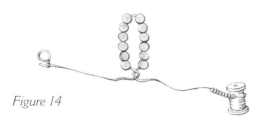

Figure 14

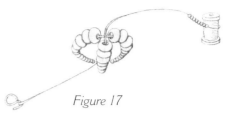

Figure 17

To make the front of the Crossover Loop, slide beads from the beaded spool Wire B toward the base of the narrowed Single Loop. Bring this beaded wire up the middle and to the top of the Loop, using just enough beads to fill in the row (Figure 15).

Figure 15

Hold these beads in place and let the extra beads on Wire B slide back toward the spool, exposing several inches of bare wire (Figure 16).

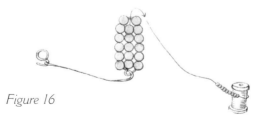

Figure 16

Cross this bare wire over the Single Loop, then press it firmly down against the exposed wire in the space between the beads at the top of the Loop. Wires will show where they cross over each other (Figure 17).

This bouquet of vintage daisies illustrates a few of the many ways to use the Loop Technique. The unknown artist's choice of color and stem beading adds richness to the composition. Collection of the author.

To make a Three-Row Crossover Loop, bring bare Wire B straight down the back of the Single Loop, stopping where you began the front row of the Crossover. Press the bare wire against the front row of the Crossover. Make sure the crossed wire stays firmly in place between the beads at the top of the Single Loop. Use the thumb and forefinger of one hand to hold the beads and the wires at the bottom of the Loop. Use your other hand to pull Wire B toward you, then wrap Wire B one time clockwise around Wire A directly below the beads. Pull the wire tight (Figure 18).

Figure 18

Use your thumbnail to push Wire B close to the base of the loop as you wrap.

To finish one Three-Row Crossover unit, swing Wire A down below the Loop and straighten it. Wrap bare Wire B around Wire A two more times in the same direction, directly below the beads. Wrap Wire B side by side, not over itself, to avoid bulky wires at the base of the Loop. Release the Loop. Leave Wire A below the Loop. Slide any remaining strung beads back toward the spool to expose a length of bare Wire B equal to the length of Wire A. Cut wire from the spool at this measurement. Be sure to knot the end of Wire B so the

beads do not slide off. Pull Wire B down below the Crossover Loop, next to Wire A. Straighten the wires and trim both ends evenly, cutting away the wire knot (Figure 19).

To make a Four-Row Crossover, bring bare Wire B partially down the back of the Loop. Use the tip of your index finger to press the bare wire against the beads where the wires cross at the top of the Loop. Angle the rest of Wire B slightly away from the Loop. Turn the Loop over so you can see the bare wire going down the back as you hold it in your hand. Slide beads from the beaded spool Wire B toward the top of the Crossover, using just enough beads to fill in the row. To keep the Crossover even, try to use the same number of beads for this back row of the Crossover as you used for the front row of the Crossover (Figure 20).

Figure 19

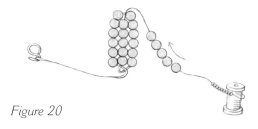

Figure 20

Press the back row of the Crossover against the front row of the Crossover to hold these beads in place. Let the extra beads on Wire B slide back toward the spool, exposing several inches of bare wire. Turn the Loop back over. Make sure the crossed wire is still firmly in place between the beads and wires at the top of the Loop (Figure 21).

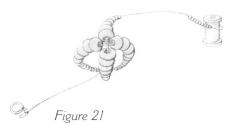

Figure 21

Use the thumb and forefinger of one hand to hold the beads and the wires at the bottom of the Loop. Use your other hand to pull Wire B toward you, then wrap Wire B one time clockwise around Wire A directly below the beads (Figure 22). Pull the wire tight.

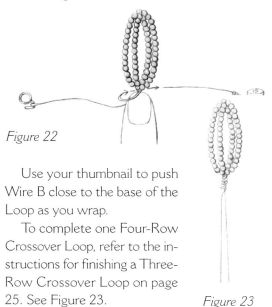

Figure 22

Use your thumbnail to push Wire B close to the base of the Loop as you wrap.

To complete one Four-Row Crossover Loop, refer to the instructions for finishing a Three-Row Crossover Loop on page 25. See Figure 23.

Figure 23

Four-Row Crossover Loop Buds

Four-Row Crossover Loops make excellent flower buds. They look charming unadorned or nestled between greenery, dancing at the end of a bouquet.

A Single Four-Row Crossover may be left as made, or twisted for a different effect. Two individual units twisted together make full buds and look best with large flowers.

Diminutive urn filled with twisted Single Four-Row Crossover Loop buds, Continuous Single Loop sepals and flat Four-Row Crossover leaves. Collection of the author.

To twist one four-row unit, hold the bottom of the Crossover Loop in one hand and the top of the Crossover Loop in the other hand. Gently turn the Loop until the rows of beads twist together. Don't twist too tightly or the beads may break or chip.

To twist two Four-Row Crossover Loops together, press the units flat, then put one on top of the other. Line them up evenly, bottom to bottom, top to top. Hold the bottoms of the loops in one hand and the tops of the loops in the other hand. Gently turn the loops as one until the rows of beads twist together.

Unless you're working with seed beads smaller than size 11°, double-unit buds have a more pleasing shape when the length of the Crossover is at least ½" before twisting.

Continuous Horizontal Loops

Continuous Horizontal Loops are the same as individual Loops except that you do not finish and cut the work from the spool until you have repeated the technique as many times as needed for the design. These Loops travel along the length of the spool wire in one direction.

Series of Single, Twisted, Figure Eight, and Crossover Loops should be made next to each other, as close together as possible. Series of Wraparounds are made not quite as close, needing space (equal to one bead length per Wrap) between them to accommodate the extra rows of beads that are wrapped around the Single Loops. (For example, two Wraps around a Single Loop means leave two bead lengths of space on the bare wire between the last complete Wraparound Loop and the beginning of the next.)

Always bend the completed Loops slightly toward the knotted end of the wire. This bend helps to keep the completed Loops out of the way as you make each successive Loop. Straighten the spool wire frequently; it's easier to make the Loops with wire that is smooth and not crimped. They'll look much nicer, too. Be consistent in the direction you turn the Loops to secure them.

Continuous Horizontal Single, Twisted, or Figure Eight Loops

To begin, make the first Loop according to the directions for constructing one unit, but do not finish it or cut it from the spool (Figure 22).

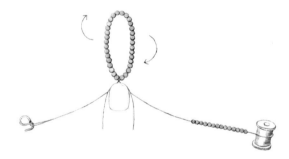

Figure 22

Once you start the series of Loops, Wire A is left alone and the work is continued with Wire B.

Close to the base of the first Loop, form a second Loop of the same size by crossing Wire B over itself directly below the beads. Do not incorporate Wire A (the knotted end of bare wire) in the second Loop. Hold the wires where they cross with the thumb and forefinger of one hand. Be sure the beads on the Loop are tight (if you're having difficulty

Make a third Loop the same way (Figure 24).

Figure 24

*Crystal snowflowers. Construction techniques in-
clude the Basic with Lacing, Continuous Single
Loops and Four-Row Crossover Loops. Collection
of the author.*

tightening the beads, you can bring them closer together by pulling Wire B to the right while you are
holding it). Turn the Loop clockwise, one time, with
your other hand. The wires will twist together, securing the second Loop (Figure 23).

Repeat the directions until you complete the required number of Loops.

To finish the unit, slide any extra beads back toward the spool to expose a length of bare Wire B
equal to the length of Wire A (Figure 25). Cut the
wire from the spool at this measurement. (Don't
forget to knot the end of spool Wire B so the remaining strung beads do not slide off.)

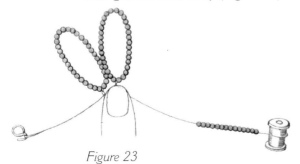

Figure 23

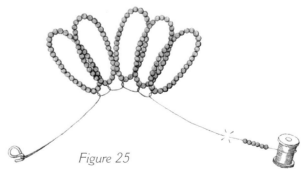

Figure 25

Bring the Loops together to form a circle by crossing Wire B over Wire A directly below the beads at the base of the Loops. (The last Loop made should be next to the first Loop of the series.) Pull the Loops up so they bunch together. Cup one hand over the unit (the tops of the Loops will face the palm of your hand) and grasp the base of the Loops with the tips of your fingers. Insert the forefinger of your other hand in the inverted **V** below the crossed wires. Hold these wires tight and use your finger to push them against the beads. Turn the Loop unit away from you to twist the two wires together (Figure 26). Continue turning the unit until

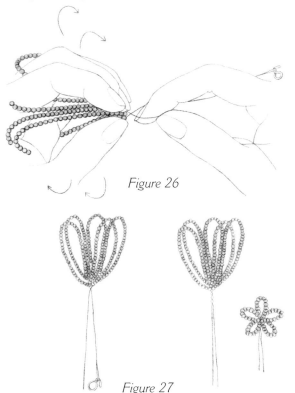

Figure 26

Figure 27

the wires are twisted for about ¼". Pull both wires down below the Loops and straighten them. Trim the ends evenly, cutting away the wire knot. Shape the Loops as desired (Figure 27).

When you are making a unit with many Loops and want one stem wire on each side of the completed circle instead of both wires on one side, weave the wires between the Loops after they are crossed instead of twisting them together (see Weaving page 57). Since weaving uses a little more stem wire than twisting, it's necessary to plan ahead and add a few extra inches to the bare wire at the beginning and the end of the unit. Cut off the wire knot so it doesn't get in the way or become tangled in the Loops. Weave one stem wire over and under the wire between the Loops all the way around the circle (back to the starting point). Use the same method to weave the other stem wire half way around the circle. Pull the stem wires down and straighten them. Pinch them together so they meet in the middle underneath the Loop unit.

For an interesting design variation when using Continuous Single Loops for a flower calyx, make two different sizes on the same wire (Figure 28).

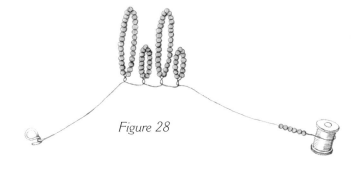

Figure 28

Continuous Wraparound Loops

The directions for Continuous Wraparound Loops and individual Wraparound Loops are the same with two exceptions. After the first Wraparound Loop of the series is completed, each additional Loop begins with Wire A in a horizontal position and is made with Wire B. Here's the way you do it.

Make the first Wraparound Loop (Loop #1) as if constructing one unit but don't finish it or cut it from the spool (Figure 29 and Figure 30).

With the work face up in front of you (Figure 30).

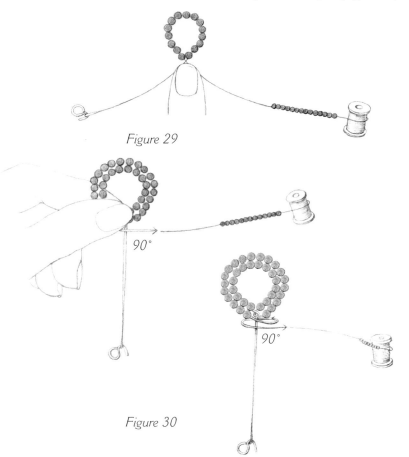

Figure 29

Figure 30

Swing Wire A up so it extends horizontally to the left of Loop #1 (Figure 31).

Figure 31

Use Wire B (cross it over itself, don't incorporate Wire A) to form the second Single Loop (Loop #2) of the Wraparound series the appropriate number of bead lengths away from Loop #1 (allow one bead length per wrap between them). Swing Wire A and Loop #1 down below Loop #2 (Wire A forms a 90° angle in relation to Wire B.) See Figure 32.

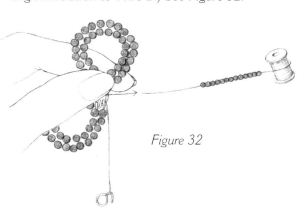

Figure 32

Wire A must be straight. Make the set of wraps around Loop #2 with Wire B (wrap it around itself, don't incorporate Wire A), then swing Wire A and Loop #1 up (horizontal) again. See Figure 33. (Wire A and the completed Wraparound Loops

Figure 33

change position each time because it's easier to make the wraps with Wire B when Wire A is below the Single Loop.)

Follow the same procedure to form the third Single Loop (Loop #3) of the Wraparound series the appropriate number of bead lengths away from Loop #2. Swing Wire A, Loop #1 and Loop #2 down below Loop #3. Make the set of wraps around Loop #3 with Wire B, then swing Wire A, Loop #1, and Loop #2 up again (Figure 34).

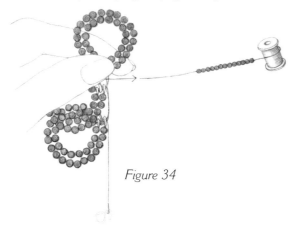

Figure 34

Continue in this manner, alternating between swinging Wire A and all completed Wraparound Loops up before forming the Single Loop and

then down before wrapping the beaded rows around it.

When you have completed the required number of Wraparound Loops, finish the unit as instructed in Continuous Single Loops.

Continuous Three- and Four-Row Crossover Loops

The directions for Continuous Crossover Loops and individual Crossover Loops are the same except that after the first Crossover Loop is completed, Wire A is left alone and the rest of the Loops in the series are made with Wire B. (Wire B is crossed over and wrapped around itself instead of over and around Wire A.) See Figure 35.

Figure 35

Make Continuous Crossover Loops one next to the other, as close together as possible. When you complete the number of Loops required for your pattern, finish the unit as instructed in Continuous Single Loops.

You can change the shape of the Continuous Four-Row Crossover Loops to make them more fully rounded. To create this fanciful "puffy" petal, put the Crossover Loop between the thumb and

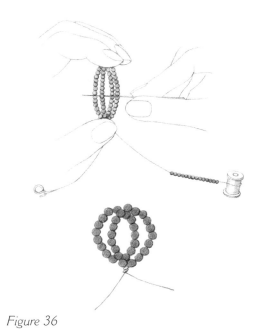

Figure 36

index finger of one hand. Make sure your fingertip is covering the top of the Loop to keep the wire firmly in place between the beads. Carefully insert the point of an awl, toothpick, or large tapestry needle into the middle of the unit. Slide the tool behind any one of the rows, then bring the point back out of the unit (like you are taking one running stitch in a length of fabric). Use the tool to gently pull the row toward you until it curves outward (Figure 36). Remove the tool. Repeat the process to curve the other rows of the unit. Still holding the Loop between your thumb and index finger, press down to compress the Loop slightly. This will round it a little bit more.

Shape all the Loops in the series one by one. It is easier to shape the Loops in this manner before they are joined into a circle.

If you want these petals to stand up higher on the wire, carefully wrap the spool Wire B around the base of each Loop twice instead of once during construction. Wrap the wire side by side. Pull it tight as you make each wrap. Use your thumbnail to push the wire wraps close to the base of the Loop to create a tiny stem.

Canterbury Bells, French, 1920s. Construction techniques include Continuous Single Loops joined and shaped with Lacing, twisted single Loops and the Basic. Silk wrapped stems. Collection of the author.

Basic Technique

Now that you have mastered the Loop Technique and the many different variations, it's time to become adept in the use of the other main French flower technique. Called the Basic, this method is the one you'll choose most often for individual leaves and flower petals.

In the beginning, if the meaning of the title of the technique seems confusing, just remember that the word Basic is used as a noun, not an adjective.

The Basic, just like the versatile Loop, has much to offer in the way of interesting design possibilities. You can make Basic units that have pointed tops and pointed bottoms; round tops and round bottoms; pointed tops and round bottoms, or vice versa.

Other variations too noteworthy not to mention include reverse wrapped wire, open Basics, and Basics that are raised, horizontal, or elongated.

Crucial to the process is your familiarity with the proper terminology and your ability to shape the wire. Once you learn these two important elements, you can begin.

Look closely at the diagram on page 35. You'll recognize some old terms you already understand (Wire Knot, Beaded Wire, and Spool Wire) and see the three new ones (Basic Count, Top Basic Wire, and Bottom Basic Loop) that are defined below.

The **Basic Count** is the center or the starting row of beads for a petal or leaf. Instructions will always mention the exact number of beads or the length of inches to use. For example, "Basic Count 3" means put three beads on the Top Basic Wire; "Basic Count ½" means to measure ½" of beads and put that amount on the wire. The remaining beaded rows of the design will be wrapped around the Basic Count. When you count the rows, always include the Basic Count as one row in the total number.

The **Top Basic Wire** is the upper single wire. The Basic Count of beads slides on this center wire. A knot on the end of the wire keeps these beads in place. The Top Basic Wire supports the beaded rows at the top of the petal or leaf. Always keep this wire straight as you work the rows around the Basic Count. If you bend it to the left or right, the petal will become crooked on one side or the other.

The **Bottom Basic Loop** is the wire below the Basic Count of Beads. It includes the portion that is twisted and the Loop. The twisted part of the wire supports the beaded rows at the bottom of the unit. When the unit is finished, the Loop becomes the stem. It is important to keep this wire straight as you work the rows around the Basic Count.

To form the Basic, slide the Basic Count of beads required for your pattern toward the knotted end of the wire. Let the remaining beads slide back toward the spool. Measure 5" of bare wire at the knotted end of the wire. Hold it between your left thumb and forefinger at this measurement. (The Basic Count should be close to the knot, temporarily out of the way.) This 5" length of wire will become the Top Basic Wire (Figure 1).

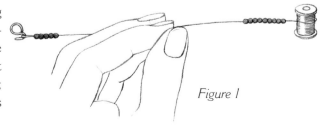

Figure 1

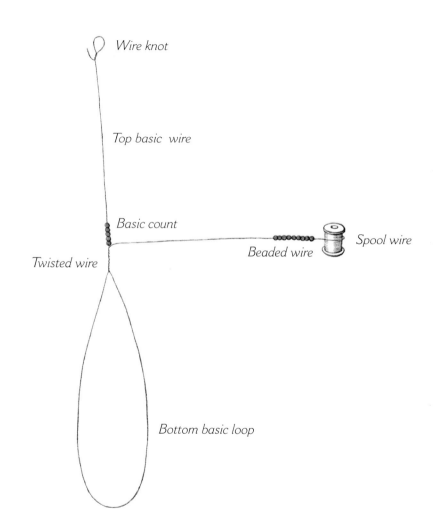

Wire knot

Top basic wire

Basic count

Twisted wire

Beaded wire

Spool wire

Bottom basic loop

Figure 2

Use your other hand to make a loop with 10" of bare spool wire. Bring this loop back to the wire you are holding in your left hand and cross the spool wire underneath the knotted wire. Shift your left fingers so you are holding both wires where they cross (Figure 2). This loop will become the Bottom Basic Loop.

Put your right forefinger in the inverted **V** below the crossed wires. Hold them tight with the other fingers of your right hand as you let go of the loop in your left hand (you are now holding the crossed wires in your right hand only). Put your left hand in the loop. Stretch your fingers, opening them wide to spread the loop and force the crossed wires against your right forefinger (Figure 3).

The loop should be tight against your left fingers and thumb. Keep your fingers wide open and turn the loop away from you by rotating your wrist and hand (the position of your hand will change from knuckles facing you to palm facing you). This one rotation of your hand will twist the crossed wires together one time. Remove your hand from the loop (do not let go of the crossed wires in your right hand). Put your left hand back in the loop with your knuckles facing you once more. Rotate the loop away from you, forcing the crossed wires to twist together again. Make sure the two wires are twisting together, not one wire wrapping around the other. Keep the twists tight and even. (This is easier to do if your left fingers are always wide open in the loop when you make the rotations.) Continue in this manner, twisting the wires until you have the same number of twists as the number of rows called for in the pattern.

Let the Basic Count slide down to rest on top of the twisted wire. (If you discover that you forgot to put the Basic Count on the Top Basic Wire before the Bottom Basic was twisted, simply snip off the wire knot, put the beads on the wire, and make another knot on the end of the Top Basic Wire.) Make sure the Top and Bottom Basic Wires are in a straight vertical line with the Top Basic

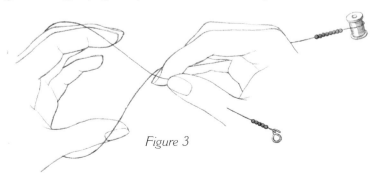

Figure 3

Wire going up (Figure 4). Place the beaded spool wire on your right and you're ready to wrap around the Basic Count the rows that make the petal round or pointed.

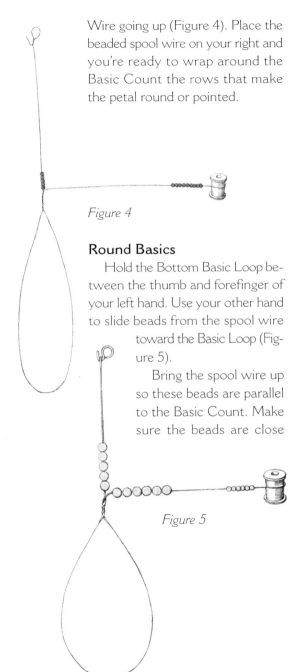

Figure 4

Round Basics

Hold the Bottom Basic Loop between the thumb and forefinger of your left hand. Use your other hand to slide beads from the spool wire toward the Basic Loop (Figure 5).

Bring the spool wire up so these beads are parallel to the Basic Count. Make sure the beads are close

Figure 5

together, filling the row completely. Too few beads will leave a space on the wire, and too many will make the row bend outward.

Push this row of beads against the Basic Count and let the remaining strung beads slide back toward the spool.

To make the petal or leaf round, the spool wire must be horizontal when it's wrapped around the Top and Bottom Basic Wires (in relation to these wires, it forms a 90° right angle). Move your fingers so you are holding both rows of beads firmly, near the top, with your left hand. Use your right hand to bring the spool wire horizontally across the front of the Top Basic Wire directly above the Basic Count (Figure 6).

Figure 6

Keep the rows of beads close together and wrap the spool wire around the back of the Top Basic Wire and horizontally across the front again. Make a complete circle around the Top Basic Wire. Use the tip of your finger to push the wrap close to the Basic Count (Figure 7).

Rotate the unit in a clockwise direction until the Bottom Basic Loop is up and the Top Basic Wire is down. Do not turn the unit over; the right side should be facing you at all times. (As soon as you

Vintage 1960s bloom. Construction techniques include the Basic and Continuous Single Loops. Creative use of color adds extra interest to the design. Collection of the author.

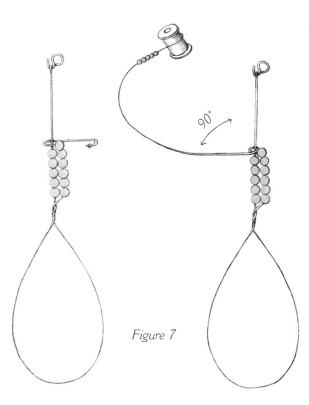

Figure 7

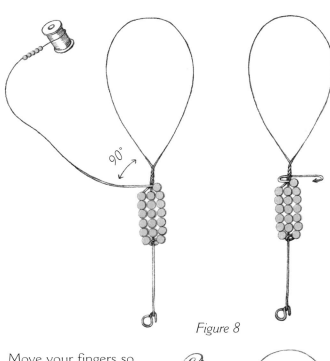

Figure 8

complete a few rows, you'll see the difference clearly because more bare wire is visible on the wrong side of the unit.) Hold the Top Basic Wire between the thumb and forefinger of your left hand (remember, this wire now points down). Use your other hand to slide beads from the spool wire toward the Top Basic Wire. Bring the spool wire up so these beads are parallel to the Basic Count. Make sure the beads are close together, filling the row completely (the beads should "kiss" where the two rows meet at the Top Basic Wire). Push this row of beads against the Basic Count and let the remaining strung beads slide back toward the spool.

Move your fingers so you are holding the rows of beads firmly, near the top, with your left hand. Use your right hand to bring the spool wire horizontally across the front of the Bottom Basic Loop where the wires are twisted above the Basic Count.

Keep the rows of beads close together and wrap the spool wire around the Bottom Basic Loop the same way you wrapped it around the Top Basic Wire (Figure 8).

You have now completed three rows of the unit. With the work still face up, turn the unit clockwise again (the Top Basic Wire is up and the Bottom Basic Loop is down) and repeat the process.

Continue in this manner, making full circles of spool wire around the Top and Bottom Basic Wires (crossing in front, going around the back, and crossing in front again) until you have the number of rows required in your pattern.

Unless otherwise directed, you will complete the last row at the Bottom Basic Loop end of the unit (remember the Loop becomes the stem). The number of rows will be uneven because the Basic Count is always included as Row 1.

There will be occasions when the beads will not precisely fill the row (one bead may extend partially over the Top or Bottom Basic Wires). When this happens, don't force the beads to fit, it's better to remove a bead from the row and then, depending on need, replace it with a smaller or larger bead from the beaded spool wire.

Design Note: While you're creating each row, stop to take a look at all the beads in the row. If a bead is too big or just oddly shaped, grasp the misshapen bead between the tips of your needle-nose pliers. Cup one hand over the tool, turn your face away, and crush the bead to remove it from the wire. Do this carefully so you don't damage or accidentally cut the wire. Slide beads from the spool toward the Basic and put back the entire row. Continue with the work. Use this method as often as needed to remove "bad" beads. The rest of the beads will fit tighter and the rows will be much neater.

To finish the Round Basic, wrap the bare spool wire two more times tightly around the Bottom Basic Loop, directly below the beads. Wrap the wire side by side, not over itself, to avoid bulk at the base of the unit. Trim the spool wire close to the last wrap. (Don't forget to knot the end of the spool wire to keep the strung beads from sliding off.) Use the tip of your needle-nose pliers to eliminate rough edges, simultaneously smoothing the cut end of the wire and curving it around the Bottom Basic Loop (Figure 9).

Figure 9

Bend the Top Basic Wire to the back (wrong) side of the unit. Trim it to about ⅛" (for smaller units) or ¼" (for larger petals or leaves). See Figure 10. Use your fingers to press the trimmed end against the beads.

Figure 10

Figure 12

Cut open the Bottom Basic Loop to make the stem wires. Trim the ends evenly and straighten both wires (Figure 11).

Figure 11

The way you cut this Loop can change the length of the stem wires. Instead of opening the bottom of the Loop, cut it open on one side or the other, just below the wrapped spool wire (Figure 12). This cut will eliminate one stem wire and make the remaining wire longer (see Reducing Wires page 64).

Pointed Basics

A pointed leaf or petal is made the same as a rounded leaf or petal except for one important change. When you wrap the spool wire around the Basic Wires, you will hold it at a 45° angle (in relation to these wires) instead of at a horizontal 90° angle. This angle makes space for the additional beads that create the point.

A petal or leaf may be round at one end (the spool wire is wrapped horizontally) and pointed at the other, or pointed at both ends. A pointed top always begins at the end of the second row and a pointed bottom at the end of the third row.

Begin with a Basic. Hold the Bottom Basic Loop between the thumb and forefinger of your left hand. Use your other hand to slide beads from the spool wire toward the Basic Loop. Bring the spool wire up so these beads are parallel to the Basic Count. Make sure the beads are close together, filling the row completely. Add to the row one more bead than you would put there if you were making a Round Basic. Push this row of beads against the Basic Count and let the remaining strung beads slide back toward the spool. Move your fingers so you are holding both rows of beads firmly, near the top, with your left hand. Use your right hand to bring the spool wire across the front of the Top Basic Wire. Hold it up at a 45° angle and wrap it around the back of the Top Basic Wire. Use the tip of your finger to push the wrap close to the Top Basic Wire (Figure 13).

Figure 13

Keep the wire in this position and let the beads from the spool slide down toward the Top Basic Wire until they rest near the last bead on the second row (Figure 14).

Hold these beads in place. Pull the spool wire down, across the front of the Top Basic Wire, bringing the beads next to the Basic Count. This movement completes the circle of spool wire around the Top Basic Wire and begins the third row. Push the beads into the point and use your fingers to flatten the spool wire against the Top Basic Wire (Figure 15).

If done correctly, the point should appear as if the first bead of the third row is sitting on top of the last bead of the second row.

Rotate the unit in a clockwise direction until the Bottom Basic Loop is up and the Top Basic Wire is down. Do not turn the unit over; the right side should be facing you at all times.

Hold the Top Basic Wire between the thumb and forefinger of your left hand. Bring the spool wire up so the beads you pulled down are parallel to the Basic Count. Make sure the beads are close together, filling the row completely.

For a pointed bottom, add one more bead to the row than you would put there if you were rounding the unit. Let any extra beads slide back toward the spool. Push this row of beads against the Basic Count. Move your fingers so you are holding the rows of beads firmly, near the top, with your left hand. Use your right hand to bring the spool wire across the front of the Bottom Basic Loop where the wires are twisted above the Basic Count.

Hold it up at a 45° angle and wrap it around the back of the Bottom Basic Loop. Use the tip of your finger to push the wrap close to the Bottom Basic Loop. Keep the wire in this position and let the beads from the spool slide down toward the Bottom Basic Loop until they rest near the last bead on the third row. Hold these beads in place. Pull the spool wire down, across the front of the Bottom Basic Loop, bringing the beads next to the Basic Count. This movement completes the circle of spool wire around the Bottom Basic Loop. Push the beads into the point and use your fingers to flatten the spool wire against the Bottom Basic Loop.

You have now completed three rows of the unit and begun the fourth row. If done correctly, the first bead of the fourth row will be sitting on top of the last bead of the third row (the first and last beads at the point always rest on top of each other). See Figure 16.

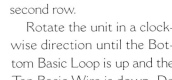

Figure 14

Figure 15

Early 1960s flowers. Construction techniques include the Basic and Twisted Four-Row Crossover Loops. Collection of the author.

Figure 16

With the work still face up, turn the unit clockwise again (the Top Basic Wire is up and the Bottom Basic Loop is down) and repeat the process.

Continue in this manner, making full circles of spool wire around the Top and Bottom Basic Wires until you have the number of rows called for in the design. To maintain the pointed effect, you must add the extra bead to every row and you must hold the spool wire at the 45° angle when wrapping it around the Basic Wires.

Unless otherwise directed, you will complete the last row at the Bottom Basic Loop end of the unit. (Remember, the Loop becomes the stem.)

The number of rows will be uneven because the Basic Count is always included as Row 1.

Finish the unit as instructed in Round Basics.

Horizontal Basics

Horizontal Basics are made the same as Round Basics with the following exceptions. There are no beads on the Top Basic Wire, narrow horizontal loops of beads form the rows, and to keep the unit symmetrical, the first two rows must be the same size. For example, if you make a twelve-bead horizontal loop on the right side of the Top Basic Wire, you must make a matching twelve-bead horizontal loop on the left side of the Top Basic Wire. There is no need to count the beads in successive rows.

Keep the rows close together and maintain the horizontal shape as you wrap around the Top and

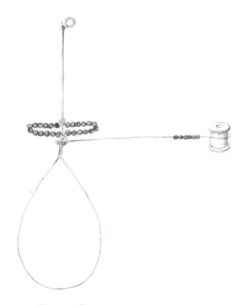

Figure 17

Bottom Basic Wires in the usual manner (Figure 17). When you've completed the required number of rows (you can count across the petal or leaf, or from the bottom up), finish the unit as instructed in Round Basics.

Dome Basics *Beehive and Button Centers*

Dome (Raised) Basics always have round tops and round bottoms. But unlike the usual Round units where the Basic Wires must be straight throughout the process, once you complete the first few rows of these units, you bend the Basic Wires at an angle. The remaining rows are wrapped around these angled wires to create a raised effect.

Beehive and Button Centers are finished at the Top Basic Wire so that you have a pair of wire extensions at both ends of the unit for support. (The Top Basic Wire and the spool wire at one end and the Bottom Basic Loop cut open at the other.) Because the last row is completed at the Top Basic Wire instead of the Bottom Basic Loop, the unit has an even number of rows.

Begin the process as if making a Round Basic. Wrap rows around the Basic Count until the flat part of the unit has reached the desired size.

To make a Beehive Center, bend both Basic

Wires down at a 45° angle. Hold the Basic Wires in this position and wrap the remaining rows around them the same way as before they were angled (Figure 18).

Rows made with the Basic Wires in this position should be slightly under each other, not side by side, and may have one or two fewer beads in them than they would if the Basic Wires were straight. Continue in this manner, making full circles of spool wire around the angled Top and Bottom Basic Wires until you have the number of rows called for in the design. Make sure you complete the last row at the Top Basic Wire.

Finish the unit by wrapping the bare spool wire two more times tightly around the Top Basic Wire close to the beads. Wrap the wire side by side, not over itself, then bring it to the end of the Top Basic Wire. When the two wires are even, cut the wire from the spool. (Don't forget to knot the end of the spool wire to keep the strung beads from sliding off.)

Cut away the wire knot from the Top Basic Wire. Cut open the Bottom Basic Loop. Trim the ends evenly and straighten the four wires (Figure 19).

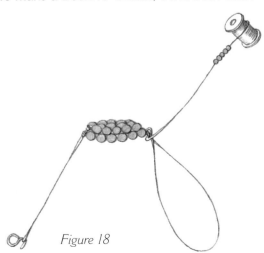

Figure 18

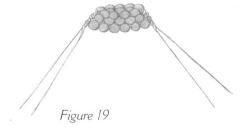

Figure 19

Construct a Button Center the same as a Beehive Center, except once you reach the desired size of the flat part of the unit, you pull the Basic Wires down to a 90° angle instead of 45° (Figure 20).

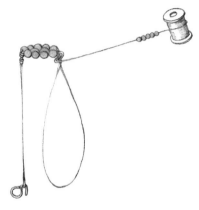

Figure 20

It's important to keep the Basic Wires in this position as you wrap the rows or the unit will get too wide.

Rows made with the Basic wires at a 90° angle are directly under each other (Figure 21). Complete the last row at the Top Basic Wire and finish the unit as instructed in Beehive Centers.

Figure 21

Elongating Basics

Sometimes you may want to elongate or sharpen the point of a petal or leaf. There are two ways to do this.

The first method is fairly simple and can be used either at the top or the bottom of the unit. Begin with a Basic. Follow the procedure for Pointed Basics, except add two extra beads to the row instead of one and hold the spool wire at a steeper angle (70°) as you wrap it around the Basic Wire. Pinch the rows together at the point to close any gaping spaces between them (Figure 22).

Figure 22

The other method is just as easy. It also looks more attractive because beads added to the Top Basic Wire fill the open space. However, it's only possible to use this method at the top of the petal or leaf. Once again, begin with a Basic. Complete the first three rows of the unit following the procedure for Pointed Basics. Cut the knot from the Top Basic Wire and add one more bead to it (Figure 23).

Wrap the spool wire around the Basic Wire in the usual manner, at a 45° angle, just above the extra bead. After completing the wrap, pinch the rows together where you added the extra bead so that a hole doesn't develop (Figure 24).

Figure 24

Figure 23

Wrap around the Bottom Basic Loop according to the regular procedure. When you reach the top of the unit, place one more bead on the Basic Wire, then wrap around it. Continue in this manner, for the required number of rows, each time adding an extra bead to the Top Basic Wire before you wrap the spool wire around it.

When you want an extremely sharp point at the tip of the petal or leaf, you can add two extra beads to the Top Basic Wire instead of only one.

Finish the elongated petal or leaf as instructed in Round Basics.

Loopback Basics

A Loopback is a combination of the Basic Technique and a lateral Single Loop. It has a Basic with a specific number of rows for the center and one or more Loops added to each side. The Loops can be the same length to match on both sides or different lengths to make the unit less uniform.

Begin with a Basic. Choose the Basic procedure you want to use for your design and make the required number of rows. Without cutting the wire from the spool, measure or count enough beads to form the first Loop of the desired size. Slide these beads toward the Bottom Basic Loop.

Bring the spool wire up so these beads are parallel to the Basic Count just as if you were making another row on the right side of the unit. Instead of making the wrap around the Top Basic Wire, bend the beaded wire into a narrow Loop and return the beaded wire to the Bottom Basic Loop.

Secure the Loop by bringing the bare spool wire across the front of the Basic Loop, around the back and to the front again between the center part of the unit and the Loop. This movement brings the spool wire to its original position at the base of the center unit to keep the bottom even when you make the next Loopback (Figure 25).

Use the same procedure to form a second Loopback on the left side of the Basic Count. Secure the Loop by bringing the bare spool wire across the

Figure 25

front of the Basic Loop, around the back and to the front again directly below the beads. Use your thumbnail to push the bottoms of both Loopbacks close to the base of the center unit (Figure 26).

Make a third Loopback on the right, directly under the first one according to the same procedure. Secure the Loop by bringing the bare spool wire across the front of the Basic Loop, around the back and to the front again between the first and third Loopback (the one just completed). This will raise the spool wire to its original position again.

Continue forming Loopbacks in this manner, always bringing the circle of spool wire to the front

Figure 26

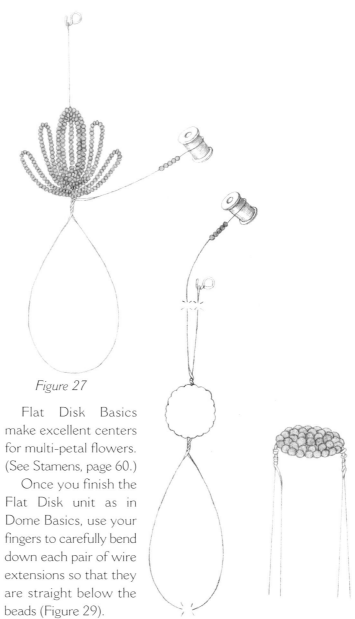

Figure 27

between the Loops on the right side of the center unit and below the beads on the left side, until you have the number of Loopbacks called for in the design (Figure 27).

Finish the unit as instructed in Round Basics.

Flat Disk Basics

Flat Disk Basics are Round Basics that are finished at the Top Basic Wire instead of at the Bottom Basic Loop (Figure 28). They have an even number of rows and a pair of wire extensions at both ends. (See Dome Basics, page 45.)

Flat Disk Basics make excellent centers for multi-petal flowers. (See Stamens, page 60.)

Once you finish the Flat Disk unit as in Dome Basics, use your fingers to carefully bend down each pair of wire extensions so that they are straight below the beads (Figure 29).

Figure 28

Figure 29

Basics with open centers (Cups)

A Basic with an open center (Cup) is mainly used for the calyx of a flower. Once the unit is completed, the petals are inserted in it. The Cup holds these pieces securely and makes an attractive finish for the bottom of the flower.

This unit is considered a Basic even though its construction is very different. It has a Top Basic Wire where it's finished, and a Bottom Basic Loop, but no Basic Count of beads. It has an even number of rows and a pair of bare wire extensions at both ends.

To make a Basic with an open center, begin by measuring 6" of bare wire at the knotted end of the spool wire. Hold it between your left thumb and forefinger at this measurement (Figure 30). This 6" length of wire will become the Top Basic Wire.

Figure 30

Slide an even number of beads from the spool toward your hand holding the wire. (These beads will become the first two rows of the unit and create the center opening for the flower petal stem wires. It's important to allow enough beads for this opening to accommodate these wires, but the open-

ing shouldn't be so big that the bottoms of the petals fall through.) Let the remaining beads slide back toward the spool.

Make a loop with 12" of bare spool wire. Bring this loop back to the wire you are holding in your left hand and cross the spool wire underneath the knotted wire. Shift your left-hand fingers so you are holding both wires where they cross. The beads you slid toward this hand should be sliding freely on this loop of wire that becomes the Bottom Basic Loop (Figure 31).

Figure 31

Put your right forefinger in the inverted **V** below the crossed wires. Hold them tight with the other fingers of your right hand as you let go of the Loop in your left hand (you are now holding the crossed wires in your right hand only). Put your left hand in the Loop. Stretch your fingers, opening them wide to spread the Loop, and force the crossed wires against your right forefinger. The Loop should be tight against your left fingers and thumb. Keep your fingers wide open and turn the Loop away from you by rotating your wrist and hand (the position of your hand will change from knuckles facing you to palm facing you). This one rotation of your hand will twist the crossed wires together one time. See Figure 32.

Make sure the two wires are twisting together, not one wire wrapping around the other. Keep the twists tight and even. (This is easier to do if your left fingers are always wide open in the Loop when you make the rotations.) Remove your hand from the Loop (don't let go of the crossed wires in your right hand). Put your left hand back in the Loop with your knuckles facing you once more. Rotate the Loop away from you, forcing the crossed wires to twist together again. Only two twists are required. (You now have a bare Top Basic Wire and a Bottom Basic Loop with an even count of beads.) Divide the beads so that an equal number is on both sides of the looped wire. Push these beads against the twisted wire. Press the beads together (Figure 33).

Use your right thumb and forefinger to hold both rows of beads firmly near the Loop wire. Put your left hand back in the Loop with your knuckles facing you. Open your fingers wide and turn the

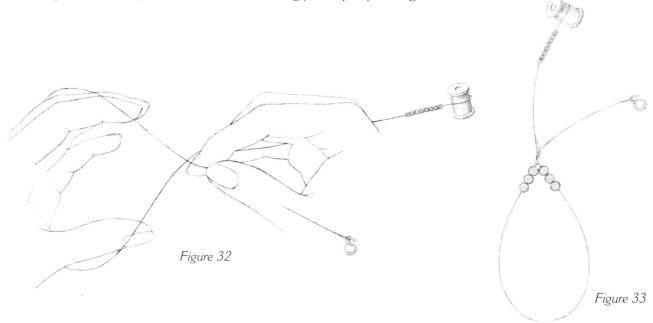

Figure 32

Figure 33

Loop away from you one time (Figure 34). This rotation will cross the Loop wires next to where

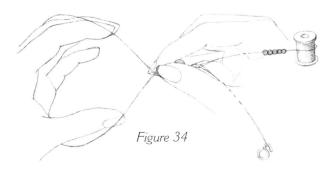

Figure 34

you are holding the beads with your right fingers. Remove your left hand from the Loop.

Move your fingers slightly forward so you are holding both rows of beads and the crossed Loop wires. Put your left hand back in the Loop and turn it away from you once more. This rotation will make the crossed Loop wires twist together one time. This twist secures the beads and completes the first two rows of the unit.

Continue holding the two rows of beads and the crossed Loop wires firmly in your right fingers and rotating the Loop with your left hand until you have the same number of twists as the number of rows called for in your design.

Insert the sharpened end of a pencil, awl, or similar round object between the two rows of beads to round them and open up the center. (These two rows take the place of the usual Basic Count of beads.) Rotate the unit in a clockwise direction until the Bottom Basic Loop is up and the Top Basic

Wire is down. Do not turn the unit over; the right side should be facing you at all times.

Make sure the Top and Bottom Basic Wires are in a straight vertical line. Place the beaded spool wire on your right and you're ready to wrap Rows 3 and 4 around the open center according to the instructions for Round Basics (Figure 35).

Figure 35

After completing the fourth row, bend both Basic Wires down at a 45° angle according to the directions for Beehive Centers (see page 45).

Wrap the remaining rows around these angled wires until you have the number of rows called for in the design. Make sure you complete the last row at the Top Basic Wire. Finish the unit as instructed in Beehive Centers. Carefully roll each pair of wire extensions over the edge of the last row of beads, threading them down into the center opening and out the bottom. Press the wires inside the unit flat against the beads (Figure 36).

Figure 36

Vintage Hibiscus. Basic Technique reinforced with Lacing. Single Loops with twisted wire stems form stamen stalk. Collection of the author.

Advanced Techniques

Lacing

The purpose of lacing is to reinforce large petals and leaves by keeping the rows of beads together, to help form and maintain the shape of some flowers made with continuous loops, and to join petals together. Lacing is done with 34-gauge wire that is wrapped around the rows of a petal or leaf between the beads.

Unless otherwise directed, always start lacing with the front side of the work facing you so that the lacing wire that shows is on the back side. The top of the petal or leaf should point up, or away from you. The procedure is the same for all purposes except that lacing to join petals together is finished in a different manner than lacing for individual petals.

To lace an individual petal or leaf, first decide where it needs to be reinforced. Some very large petals and long slender leaves may require more than one row of lacing to support them. Cut a length of 34-gauge wire approximately two times the width of the area to be laced, plus comfortable working ends (about 5"–6" extra). Begin on the right-hand side of the petal or leaf. Insert one end of the lacing wire from the front between the first

and second rows of the petal and push 3" to the back side. Hold both ends of the wire and pull them to the right until the wire bends around the first row and is caught between two beads. The long end of the wire is on top of the row (Figure 1).

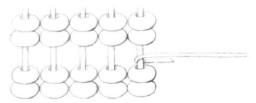

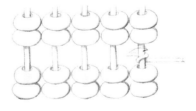

Figure 1

Secure the lacing wire by wrapping the long end around the outside of Row 1, then bring it up to the front between the first and second rows. Wrap the wire around the outside of Row 1 once more, but this time bring it up to the front between Rows 2 and 3. Wrap the wire around Row 2 and bring it up to the front between Rows 3 and 4. Wrap the wire around Row 3 and bring it up to the front

Vintage Calla Lily. Basic Technique reinforced with multiple rows of Lacing. Jewelled stems and coiled stamen. Collection of the author.

between Rows 4 and 5. Continue in this manner until all rows are laced together (Figure 2).

Be sure to keep the rows close together by pulling the lacing wire toward you each time you come up to the front between the rows. You can't pull them together after you have laced the row.

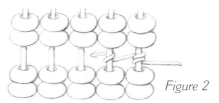

Figure 2

Keep the wraps tight and between the beads and the lacing wire as straight as possible. If you have difficulty pushing the wire between the rows, thread the wire through a tapestry needle to help you move forward across the petal. End the lacing by wrapping the last row twice. Trim the lacing wire on each side of the petal to ⅛". Use the tip of your needle-nose pliers to curve this wire toward the front; hide the ends between the beads (Figure 3).

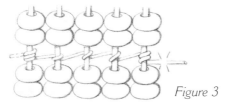

Figure 3

If the wire breaks before you complete the lacing, estimate the length of wire needed to finish the work. Attach this new piece of wire with a double wrap where the old wire broke and continue. Trim

the ends of both wires to ⅛" and hide them between the beads.

Use this same method of lacing to join petals together. After deciding where the petals are to be joined (near the top or bottom, or through the middle), begin as before and lace across the front to the last row of the first petal. Wrap around this row only once. Place the first row of the second petal next to the last row of the first petal and continue lacing, treating the second petal as a continuation of the first one. Make sure all the tops of the petals are even (Figure 4). Repeat the process until you've joined the required number of petals.

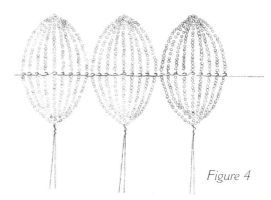

Figure 4

To close the flower and join the petals, put the last petal next to the first petal where you began the lacing (right sides facing in or right sides facing out depending upon the design of the flower). Bring the lacing wire up to the front between the first and second rows of the first petal, just as if you were going to lace another row, but do not wrap the wire around the row. Pull the lacing wire toward you to draw the petals close. Hold the petals together. Wrap the lacing wire around the last row of the last petal, then bring it up to the front one more time between the first and second rows of the first petal so it meets the short length of wire where the lacing began. (This time you are wrapping the lacing wire around two rows instead of one row.) Take the ends of both lacing wires and cross one over the other close to the beads. Twist them together three or four times to secure the lacing. Trim both ends close to the twisted wires. Use your needle-nose pliers to tuck the twisted wires between the beads (Figure 5).

Figure 5

Rows of Continuous Loops may be shaped and joined with lacing. To begin, narrow the Loops slightly (see Single Loops page 19). The narrowing will help keep the Loops close together as you lace them. Place the unit face up, with Loops at the top and evenly spaced. Decide how far down from the top of the Loops to lace and begin as before on the right-hand side of the Loops. Secure the lacing wire to the first row of the first Loop and lace across the front to the last row of the last Loop. You can wrap the lacing wire around every row of every Loop or skip one row of each Loop. In the latter case, more

bare lacing wire is visible across the back side of the Loops (Figure 6).

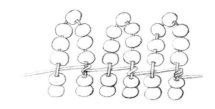

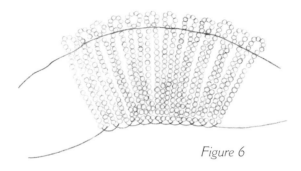

Figure 6

To join the last Loop to the first Loop to close the flower and end the lacing, follow the same finishing instructions for joining two or more petals together. The tip of the loops above the lacing may be left narrowed or made rounder by inserting the point of a sharpened pencil or an awl carefully through the opening.

Weaving

Weaving is another way to keep a flower in a particular shape. This method is used less frequently than lacing because petals that are woven to hold their shape are not as sturdy as those that are laced.

To weave petals or leaves together, cut a length of 34-gauge wire about two or three times the width of the area to be woven plus comfortable working ends. Decide where to weave (top or bottom, or through the middle) and secure one end of the wire as if you were going to lace the petal or leaf. Then simply weave the wire in and out of the rows of each petal, adding petal or leaf units as you weave, until you reach the starting point. You may put the petals next to each other or overlap them slightly. Keep the wire straight and between the beads.

Pull the weaving wire as tightly as you desire the flower to close, then hold the wire in place by wrapping it around the row where you started. Take the ends of both weaving wires and cross one over the other close to the beads. Twist them together three or four times to secure the weaving. Trim both ends close to the twisted wires. Use your needle-nose pliers to tuck the twisted wires between the beads.

You can also use weaving to make a circle of continuous loops. This method is especially effective if you are making large flowers or flowers with many layers. Weave the stem wires over and under between the loops until they are opposite one another instead of twisted together on one side of the circle (see Continuous Loops, page 27).

Reverse Wrap

Use the Reverse Wrap whenever you want the wire that shows on the wrong side of a petal or leaf

to be on one half of the unit on one side and on the other half of the unit on the opposite side. For example, a petal or leaf made in the usual manner has wire that shows on one side only. If you shape the petal or leaf by rolling the top half sharply back, the wire on the wrong side at the tip doesn't show, but the wire on the wrong side at the bottom half will be very visible when the flower is assembled (Figure 7).

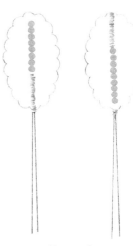

Figure 7

If you use the Reverse Wrap at the bottom when you make the petal or leaf, the wire that shows will still be at the bottom, but on the opposite side. To clarify this further, one side of your petal will have a right side at the top and a wrong side at the bottom. The other side of the same petal will have a wrong side at the top and a right side at the bottom (Figure 8).

When the flower is assembled, the wrong side (where the wire shows) at the bottom of the petal or leaf is placed against the main stem facing inward (the right side faces

Figure 8

Figure 9

out). This arrangement hides the wire at the bottom of the unit; the wire at the top is not noticeable because it's concealed by the curved shape (Figure 9).

A Reverse Wrap is fairly simple to do. Make the rows of the Basic as usual and wrap the spool wire in reverse around one Basic Wire or the other, just as the name suggests. Instead of wrapping it front to back to front, you wrap it back to front to back (Figure 10).

You can Reverse Wrap at either end of a petal or leaf and use the method to make units that are round or pointed. However, it is easier to execute the maneuver at the Bottom Basic where the twisted Loop wires offer more support or at the round end of a unit when the other end is pointed because it can be difficult to maintain the point and Reverse Wrap at the same time (Figure 11).

If a unit requires both Lacing and Reverse Wrapping, make sure the wires that show are on the same side.

Figure 11

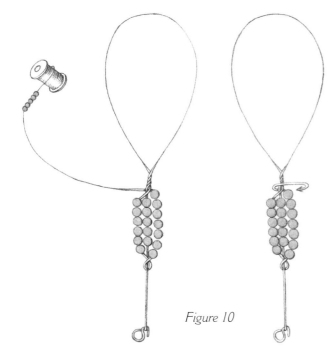

Figure 10

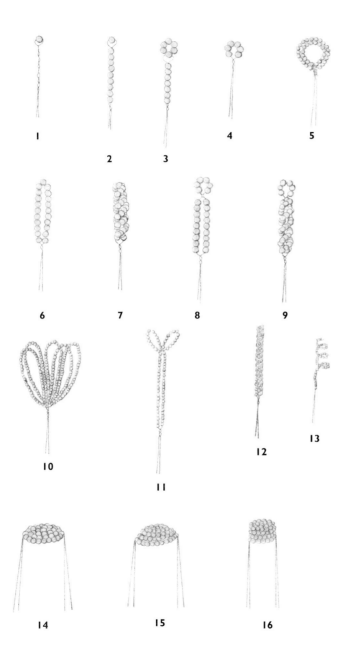

1
2
3
4
5
6
7
8
9
10
11
12
13
14
15
16

Flower Centers (Stamens)

Stamens in various forms and lengths can transform the look of your flower.

Twist a single bead in the middle of a folded wire, let just a few such wires peek over the edges, and the effect will be delicate and airy.

When you want the stamens to make a stronger statement, multiple continuous loops are quite impressive nestled deep in the center of a blossom. A flat beaded disk, one large single bead, or a slender jeweled stalk—all can quickly change the character of the flower.

As you consider the numerous design possibilities, don't forget that the color of the beads you choose for your stamens also plays a part in bringing your blooms to life. Yellows and oranges are common, a bright green or black less ordinary. Dare to venture beyond the obvious. Contrast matters. Stamens are rarely the same hue as the flower; even nature has its surprises. What will make your flowers glorious are the little accents of color you use with them.

Flower Center Ideas

1. Single bead in the middle of a folded twisted wire. May be used by itself or clustered.

2. Single bead threaded on wire that has been folded with additional beads threaded on both wires to form a single strand. Strands may be clustered. *Design option:* Use a large bead on top and small beads for the strand.

3. Loop of beads above a single strand of beads.

4. Single loop of beads.

5. Wraparound loop of beads.

6. Longer single loop of beads pressed together.

7. Single loop of beads pressed together and twisted.

8. Loop of beads above additional beads strung on each wire.

9. Loop of beads, double strand twisted.

10. Five continuous loops of beads joined together on one wire.

11. Two continuous loops above beads strung on each longer wire. *Design option:* Double strand of beads may be twisted.

12. Single strand of beads spiraled around a tapestry needle or round toothpick, coils pushed close together.

13. Single strand of beads coiled loosely around a pencil, wire end above last bead wrapped around a needle to make a tendril, then trimmed.

14. Flat disk, Basic Technique

15. Beehive center, Basic Technique

16. Button center, Basic Technique

To use any one of the Basic Technique centers, you can bring the bare wire extensions together and insert them in the opening in the middle of the flower. You can also place the bare wire extensions over the outside edge between two petals (on opposite sides), then bend them so they meet in the middle under the flower.

Flower Assembly

Figure 1

Figure 2

NOW THAT YOU HAVE learned the various techniques for making flower petals, leaves, and stamens, it's time to use your skills and a touch of originality to put all the parts and pieces together. Most instruction books for making flowers will tell you to stack or layer the pieces and twist the stem wires to hold them together. This sounds simple, but it's not always easy to hold the many parts in place and neatly twist the wires at the same time. Petals tend to slip and shift and the twists become uneven. Twists that are uneven make the stems lumpy. Lumpy stems are difficult to hide and a graceful looking flower is no longer possible.

In contrast, I assemble all my flowers without twisting wires below the parts at all. When you use either one of my two methods with the various stem coverings, your stems will turn out perfectly and you'll never have to worry that a flower will come apart.

My favorite way to hold petals together is to use a calyx. In this instance, the calyx is not a ring of individual sepals that surround the outside of a flower or bud. It is, instead, a small circle of Continuous Loops (Figure 1) or a Cup made using the Basic Technique (Figure 2); this circle or cup cradles the bottom of the flower.

Let the flower guide your choice of calyx, then simply insert the stem wires into the center opening of this separate unit. (If you're stacking Continuous Loop units to make a flower, it's not always necessary to make a separate calyx. The last Loop unit will serve the same purpose even though it may not be green.) Space the petals and any stamen evenly. Make sure the pieces are nestled snugly within the calyx. Straighten the stem wires below the beads and you're ready to finish the flower.

When I use this method to assemble a flower, my next step is to cover the stem wires with my choice of thread, cording, or beads. I never use assembly wire to bind the main stem wires below the calyx. It's not necessary. The petals are held in place by the calyx and you can hold the stem wires, add buds or leaves as desired, then wrap them together with your covering all at the same time.

It may take some practice until you can do this easily. If your first attempts seem awkward, use transparent tape to bind the stem wires temporarily. Remove the tape when you come to it as you wind the thread or beads down the stem.

When a separate calyx is not appropriate for a

flower, I use 34-gauge lacing wire to bind the petals together. If the flower has many pieces, it's best to put them together one at a time. If you are working with just two or three petals, you can hold them tightly enough to bind them together all at once.

Unwind about 12" of the wire but do not cut it from the spool. Take the end of the wire and insert 2" between the beads at the base of the unit that will be the flower's center. Make sure the wire is hidden between these beads, then bend the 2" end down the stem (Figure 3).

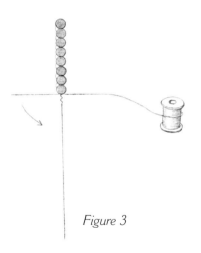

Figure 3

Wrap the assembly wire one time around the center unit, winding it over itself to secure it to the stem. Pull the assembly wire tight, then bind on the remaining petals one at a time.

Make sure the bottoms of the petals are even. Don't let them slip down the stem unless you want them that way. It's not necessary to wrap around each one more than once because you are encircling all the petals every time you add one to the flower. Overlap and stagger the pieces as desired.

When you assemble a small flower or bud with two or three pieces you can bind them in a cluster. Place the petals around the center unit. Hold them together with one hand and use the other hand to wrap the assembly wire around them all at the same time.

Keep the assembly wire close to the base of the flower, wrapping it tightly over itself each time, directly below the beads. You'll know you're wrapping tight enough if you can let go of everything and the flower stays together.

The last few petals or individual sepals can be drawn in closer to the bottom of the flower if you carefully bend each unit down at its base and cup it slightly before binding it to the flower. You will bend these units up later when you shape the flower (Figure 4).

Once you have bound all the parts together, wrap the assembly wire once more around the base of the flower, directly below the beads.

Figure 4

To avoid any risk of having the assembly wire loosen later, do not cut it from the spool. Instead, wind the wire down the entire length of the stem. If you need to taper the stem wires, you must trim them before you wrap the assembly wire completely down the stem.

Keep the stem wires straight and the wraps evenly spaced (about $\frac{1}{16}$" apart) as you bring the wire to the bottom of the stem.

Cut the assembly wire from the spool. Use your fingers or the tip of your needle-nose pliers to curl the end of the assembly wire around the bottom of the stem, and you're ready to finish the flower with your choice of stem covering.

Reinforcing Stems

As a general rule, stems need to be reinforced to help support large flowers or heavy flowers with many petals. Stems wrapped with beads and those covered by large stem beads may also require extra strengthening. When necessary, stems should be reinforced with a piece of heavy-gauge support wire (18, 20, or 22 gauge) after the flower head is assembled.

Select the gauge strong enough to do the job, but not more than needed. Cut this wire to match the length of the stem. Put the support wire next to the stem wires. Push one end up against the bottom of the flower, directly below the beads. Wiggle the wire so it disappears into the other stem wires. From this point on, treat the support wire as part of the stem. (You can hold the wire in place or attach it temporarily with a piece of transparent tape.) Continue to finish the flower the same as you would have without the reinforcing wire.

Lengthening Stems

You can also use a support wire to lengthen a stem that is too short. Fan out the ends of the main stem wires. Taper the ends of these wires by cutting them off at different lengths (see page 65).

Select the correct gauge support wire. Cut the additional length needed to make the stem longer, plus ½". Put the support wire next to the tapered stem wires and wiggle it a bit so the extra ½" disappears into these ends.

Use your fingers to press the trimmed ends back in place. Run your fingers down the wires to check the smoothness of the stem. If it feels too thin below where you added the extra length, cut another piece of support wire and add it to the stem. Build up the stem in this manner until it feels smooth and even. You can hold the additional wire in place or attach it temporarily with a piece of transparent tape. Then complete the flower the same as you would have without the additional length of stem wire.

Reducing Wires

Sometimes it's necessary to eliminate bare stem wires from flower petals or parts before they are assembled. The need can be for aesthetic purposes only or to make it possible to use seed beads on the stems of leaves, buds, and other individual units.

Whatever the reason for reducing these wires, in all cases, the stem will be thinner. To reduce wires, take one bare stem wire in each hand. Pull them gently until they are spread slightly apart at the base of the unit. If the two stem wires are twisted below the beaded unit, you may cut away either one of the two. Cut it just below the last twist (Figure 5).

If the two stem wires below the unit are wrapped, one around the other, you must trim the wire that wraps around the straight wire (a trimmed, straight wire is less secure). Cut it just below the last wrap (Figure 6).

Figure 5   Figure 6

Figure 7

When you are working with a unit that is constructed using the Basic Technique (see page 34), you may cut away either one of the two wires that was a side of the Bottom Basic Loop. (The spool end of the wire will have been trimmed already.) Cut the wire just below the wrapped spool wire. If the bottom Basic Loop has not yet been cut open, you can reduce the two wires to one and lengthen the remaining stem wire at the same time (Figure 7).

Always cut only one stem wire. Use your fingers to push the trimmed end back against the remaining stem wire so it doesn't stick out.

Tapering Stem Wires

Tapering stem wires is different from reducing stem wires. When you reduce wires, you bluntly cut off the full length of one bare wire at the base of a flower petal or part. When these pieces are assembled later, the overall stem is thinner. When you taper wires, you trim many wires at different lengths to gradually thin the main stem of a flower that has already been assembled. Although both methods serve the same purpose (to thin stems), there are different reasons to use one method over the other. For example, you may choose to taper wires if the main stem is becoming bulky below added foliage or to avoid a blunt stem end.

You must taper wires at the bottom of the main stem before adding a support wire to lengthen the stem or prepare it for stem beading that is combined with wrapped beading. To taper wires, simply fan them out and cut them off at varying lengths wherever they need to be trimmed. Unless you are tapering the stem in preparation to lengthen or stem bead it (see page 69), leave a few wires untrimmed to maintain the full stem length desired (Figure 8).

Figure 8

Use your fingers to press the tapered wires back in place. Run your fingers down the wires to check the smoothness of the stem. If they need no further trimming, finish the stem the same as you would have without the tapered wires.

Stem Coverings

The earliest flowers that I have collected have stems that are elegantly wrapped with threads of silk or sumptuously embellished with beads. The stems of today's beaded flowers should be ornamented, too. Since I am partial to lush coverings, my instructions will always tell you how to duplicate the elaborate finishes on my vintage works of art.

You'll learn ways to wrap stems with silk thread or beads exactly like the antique pieces and imitate the costly appearance of silk with floss or cording. These materials will not only give the stems a rich decorative finish, but as an added benefit, they'll make your flowers more visually interesting.

Embroidery Floss

Embroidery floss is a perfect choice of covering when you want a stem finish that is similar in style to the more expensive strands of silk. It is a versatile thread suitable for the stems of all types and sizes of beaded flowers and foliage, and it often adds just the right touch of necessary sophistication to your bouquets.

You will be pleased how easy it is to achieve superb results with this thread wrapped around stems the vintage way described below. Before you

begin, it's important to know that covering stems with embroidery floss can serve two useful purposes. Several strands (plies) wrapped around the bare wires can be a foundation covering that prepares the stem for a final finish of beads, cord, or another wrap of floss. This color background hides wire that might show through the other coverings if they were used alone.

Preliminary wraps with floss are best when used on main flower stems only; it is seldom necessary to prepare the smaller stems of other foliage in this manner. Floss can also be the final finish when one wrapping with thread is sufficient to cover the bare stem wires.

It makes no difference whether the floss is a foundation for other coverings or a final stem finish; the procedure itself is simple and the technique you use to apply it is the same. Begin with a length of floss cut about six or seven times longer than the stem. This may be more floss than you need, but it's better to be generous—you can always trim. To keep the floss from tangling, it helps to divide the skein in half, then gently ease out the threads and separate them one at a time.

Allow each strand to untwist. Smooth them between your fingers, then put them back together. This takes a little extra time, but the floss is easier to work with when you separate the strands and they really do stay smoother as you wind them around the stem. Use about three strands of floss for a preliminary wrap; you don't want to make the stem bulky. When the floss is the final stem finish, use as many strands as required to ensure thorough coverage.

Be sure the stem is ready to be wrapped, all wires

neatly tapered and extra ones reduced, as necessary. Carefully bend down one petal, loop, or sepal on the outside of the flower. Take the end of the floss (treating all the strands as one) and slip it over the petal. Slide the floss down toward the base of the flower until it rests on top of the wires directly below the beads at the bottom of the petal (Figure 9).

Figure 9

Pull the floss so one end extends about 2" down the stem. Work the floss back and forth until it catches on the wires. Return the petal to its original position.

If you assembled the flower with a separate cup calyx, insert the floss between the first and second row of beads at the bottom of the calyx. Slide the floss close to the flower stem, then pull one end down about 2". Make sure the floss rests on top of the wire, hidden between two beads in the first row (Figure 10).

Figure 10

When the part to be covered is the stem of a leaf constructed with the Basic Technique, push the floss between the first and second row of beads at the base of the unit. Slide the floss next to the stem wires, then pull one end down about 2". Make sure the floss rests on top of the wire, hidden between beads in the first row (Figure 11).

If the leaf is made with Continuous Loops, insert the floss through a Loop near the stem wires. Pull the floss down about 2", making sure it rests on top of the twisted wires between the beads at the base of the Loop (Figure 12).

Dab a little glue on the stem with a toothpick. Hold the 2" end of the floss down the stem with one hand. Use your other hand to wrap the floss around the

Figure 11

Figure 12

Figure 13

stem, winding it over itself, close to the bottom of the flower as you begin. Wrap the floss around the stem, laying the strands side by side. Keep the thread smooth and spread flat as you move it down the stem (Figure 13).

Every now and then, put a little glue on the stem to hold the floss in place. If you have difficulty keeping the wraps smooth and even, it sometimes helps to slowly twirl the stem with one hand and hold the floss taut with the other hand. Keep the stem wires straight. Stop winding the floss periodically to allow the strands to untwist.

If you find you're running out of floss before you complete the wrapping, wind the last bit of floss diagonally down the stem for about 1". Glue the end to the stem. Cut another length of floss long enough to finish the wrapping. Glue this new floss to the stem where the old floss was wrapped diagonally, with the end pointing down. Bring the new floss up and use your thumbnail to press it next to the last "straight" wrap of the old floss (above the diagonal thread). Pull the new floss tight. Wrap it around the stem, winding it over itself as you start out. Dab a little glue on the stem to keep the floss in place and continue wrapping the stem.

When you are near the length desired, cut any straggly wire ends off evenly. Put some glue on the bottom of the stem wires and wind the floss around them. Use the tip of your finger (like you're covering the end of a straw) to hold the floss in place for a few seconds, then wind the floss back up the stem for about ¼". Trim the floss and dab a

little glue on the ends. Use your fingers to smooth them against the stem.

It's a good idea to add buds or leaves to the main flower stem only during the final wrapping with floss. This allows you to make last minute adjustments to the flower and prevents the floss from tangling in the foliage. Join the buds or leaves to the main flower stem as you come to their position. Hold the pieces in place or attach them temporarily with transparent tape. Wrap the floss tightly around both stems at the same time.

When totally wrapped stems of foliage add too much bulk to the main flower stem, cover just the length needed and leave the rest of the stem wires unfinished. For example, if you want a leaf to extend 1" from the main flower stem, wrap the bare wires for that measurement. End the floss wrapping in the same manner as if you ran out of thread. Put the unit next to the main flower stem. Hold it so that you wrap the floss around the unfinished wires below the 1" stem extension as you bind the unit close to the main stem (Figure 14).

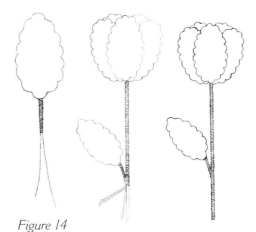

Figure 14

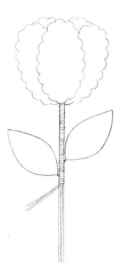

Figure 15

Figure 16

You can omit floss wrapping from foliage stems if you join these pieces right next to the main flower stem (Figure 15).

To attach a leaf or bud with a beaded stem, put the unit's bare stem wires next to the main flower stem slightly above its final position. (Some bare wire will be visible above the floss that was already wrapped around the main flower stem.) Don't be concerned if the stem beads loosen. Wrap the floss around the bare stem wires and the main flower stem at the same time for about ¼". (Your first wrap around both stems will not cover all the visible bare wire beneath the stem beads.) Put a little glue on the main flower stem to keep the floss in place. Hold the main flower stem with one hand and gently pull down the unit's bare stem wires with the other hand. The unit's stem will slide in place, close to the floss wrapping. The loose beads will tighten and the bare wire near the join will disappear (Figure 16).

Press the bare wires that you pulled against the main flower stem and continue with the floss wrapping.

Silk Floss

To finish the stems of your beaded flowers exactly like vintage ones, choose stranded silk thread. Apply it to the stems the same as embroidery floss and use it for both preliminary and final stem coverings.

To achieve the best results, use glue very sparingly so it doesn't bleed through the strands. Keep your nails and hands as smooth as possible to prevent snags. Once the skein is opened, the silk has a tendency to tangle, so wrap the strands around a small square of cardboard or an empty thread spool until you are ready to use it.

After you have wrapped the stems, look to see if there has been any fuzzing of the filaments. Clip them carefully without cutting the thread.

Nylon Cord

Nylon cord is a striking covering for the main stems of all flowers and the stems of other beaded foliage as well. You'll use this cord as sized, directly from the spool. It lends itself beautifully as a final stem finish, but because it's rather thick (about ½mm diameter), it's usually unsuitable for a preliminary wrap-use floss for that instead. For a final stem finish, follow the same procedure when using nylon cord as you would embroidery floss.

Beaded Stems

The beauty of many flowers is enhanced when the stems are jeweled with beads in contrasting or matching colors. Be extravagant and wrap the entire stem with small seed beads strung on lacing wire. String large seed beads directly on the main flower stem when size permits. Put small seed beads on the stems of leaves and tiny flowers for another charming look. Try combinations of all these methods to obtain dazzling results. To determine which method to choose, keep in mind the size and nature of the flower and how it will be used when it is finished.

For wrapped beaded stems, select a bead size and color that complements the flower. The bead most commonly used for this purpose is a size 11° seed bead, but don't hesitate to experiment with smaller or larger sizes. Prepare the stem by covering it with embroidery floss that matches or blends with the beads you have selected. Buds, leaves, and small flowers should be added as you wrap the floss around the stem. You will jewel around them when you wrap the stem with the beaded wire.

After wrapping with floss, string beads equal to at least three or four times the length of the stem on 34-gauge lacing wire and knot the end. Pick up the spool and slide the beads back toward it to expose 3"–4" of bare wire. Bend the end of the wire to form a hook. Cut away the wire knot.

Carefully pull down one petal or sepal on the outside of the flower. Slip the hook over this petal or sepal. Slide it down toward the base of the flower until the hook rests on top of the wires directly below the beads at the bottom of the petal. (If the flower has a separate cup calyx unit, slip the hook over the first row of beads closest to the stem. Then make sure the wire goes between two beads.) See Figure 17.

Figure 17

Bend the petal back up toward the flower. Use your fingers to pinch the hook closed. Hold the short end of the wire hook next to the stem with one hand. Use your other hand to wrap the bare spool wire over itself and around the stem two times, close to the beads at the bottom of the flower. Pull the spool wire tight. Push beads from the spool toward the bottom of the flower and wrap the stem with the beaded wire. Keep the beads on the wire close together and the beaded rows next to each other as you wind down the stem. If you have difficulty keeping the rows close together, it may help to twirl the flower with one hand and maintain the tension of the beads with your other hand (Figure 18).

Figure 18

When you reach the point where leaves or buds are joined, be sure to wrap carefully to avoid gaps between the rows. Continue wrapping the full length of the stem. To end the wrapping, push any remaining beads back toward the spool to expose a length of bare wire. Wrap the bare wire around the end of the stem two or three times. Pull the wire tight. Cut the wire from the spool. Hide the cut end by pushing it up under the last two rows of beads with your fingers or the tip of your needle-nose pliers.

If you run out of beads before completing the wrapping, cut a length of bare wire from the spool long enough to finish. Add beads to the cut end and knot the wire. Continue wrapping to the end of the stem. Cut the wire knot away and hide the cut end under the last two rows of beads as previously instructed.

You can use large size seed beads (sizes 8°, 6°, and occasionally 4°) to cover main flower stems. Once you choose an appropriate size and color, simply add the beads to the stem one by one. Push them from the bottom of the stem wire, or wires, up to the base of the flower or calyx until you have covered the full length of the stem. Use a dab of glue to secure the last bead in place (Figure 19).

Figure 19

Flowers with stems beaded in this manner are often bound together in clusters and planted in a container. To make such an arrangement, leave several inches of the lower section of every stem unfinished. Group the pieces with the stem beads at the bottom lined up evenly. Use a piece of transparent tape to temporarily bind them together. Then wrap these bare wires as if they were one unit with floss, cord, or beaded wire.

Stem beading with the large size seed beads is a grand embellishment, but it does have one drawback. It's most successful only when flowers have slender stems without any foliage. These beads seldom fit on a thick stem. And if they do fit, when the stem has foliage, the beads frequently settle unevenly next to the buds or leaves that are bound to the stem. This doesn't look pretty.

If you are willing to forego attached foliage, and large beads fit, be sure the finished stem is in proportion to the flower. If you narrow a stem you know will be too large by reducing wires before assembling the petals, take care that the stem can support the flower.

When you want to use beads for a stem finish and all else fails, the best solution is to combine wrapped beading with stem beading. Here's how to do this easily.

After assembling the flower head (see page 62), taper the stem wires (see page 65) near where you want to begin stem beading. Choose a suitable gauge of stem support wire and make sure the stem beads you want to use will fit on it. Add the support wire to the tapered stem wires just as if you were lengthening the stem (see page 64).

Prepare the portion of the stem that will be wrapped with beads by covering it with embroidery floss. Use the floss to bind on any buds or leaves (see page 68). Be sure to keep this foliage above the support wire.

Stop winding the floss when you are near the tapered ends of the wires. Run your fingers down these wires to check the smoothness of the stem. You want to make a neat transition from the tapered ends to the support wire that is now the main flower stem. When the stem feels nice and even, continue to wind the floss down the stem. Finish the floss wrapping on the new main flower stem, about ½" beyond the bottom of the tapered stem wires. Trim the floss and dab a little glue on the ends. Use your fingers to smooth these ends around the stem.

Following the instructions for wrapped beaded stems (see page 70), wrap the beaded wire below the flower head and down the tapered stem area. Stop the bead wrapping just slightly above where the floss covering ends on the main flower stem. Slide any extra beads back toward the spool to expose a few inches of bare wire. Wrap this bare wire over the glued ends of the floss and down the uncovered portion of the main stem wire for about 1".

Keep the wire tight as you wind it around the stem. Cut the wire from the spool and curve the end around the stem with your fingers. Add stem beads to the uncovered main stem wire one by one. Nestle the first bead close to the last row of wrapped beading and make sure the next few beads go over the end of the bare 34-gauge wire. Add beads until you have covered the full length of the stem (Figure 20). Use a dab of glue to secure the last bead in place.

Figure 20

Stem Beading with Small Seed Beads

Small seed beads (size 11° and 10°) make an attractive stem finish for leaves, buds, simple loop flowers, and other beaded units.

There are several ways to do this stem beading. Each of the following methods has its unique characteristics plus optional design treatments. The one you choose will lend personal style to your creation.

For a single beaded stem, bring together the two bare wires at the base of the unit, then feed the beads one by one on the bottom of the stem. For a stem that looks the same when the beads do not fit on both wires easily, reduce one wire (see page 64) and string the beads on the wire that remains.

Push the beads up to the base of the unit. Stop when you reach the length desired. In most instances, this will be the distance you want the unit to extend from the main flower stem. Put a piece of transparent tape around the wire left bare to hold the beads in place until you are ready to use the unit (Figure 21).

Once the stem is beaded you can leave it straight or coil it loosely around a pencil or small dowel. When the dowel is removed, the unit will bend and sway, adding graceful movement to the stem (Figure 22).

Figure 21

It's also possible to make a small grouping with two or three of these stem-beaded units. Remove the transparent tape. Bundle the pieces, right sides facing you, stem beads at the bottom lined up evenly. Make sure the beads are tight. Cup your hand over the units (they should be facing the palm of your hand), then use your thumb and forefinger to hold the bare wires together directly below the stem beads. Simultaneously grasp these same bare wires with your other hand (your fingers should be about ¼" apart). Turn the wires away from you, twisting them together all at the same time. Don't let the units in your cupped hand slip out of position. Twist the wires for about ¼", then taper the ends of the wires left bare below the twist. Once you press the tapered ends back in place, the cluster is ready to be bound to the main flower stem (Figure 23).

For another interesting effect, try using a large

Figure 22

Figure 23

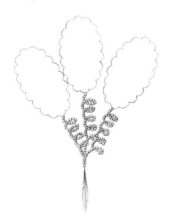

seed bead to make a calyx. Push this bead on the bare wires first, then add the smaller beads to the stem.

For an entirely different effect, you can make a two-strand beaded stem. Simply string beads on each end of the bare wires and push them up to the base of the unit, one by one. When the beaded portion of the stem is long enough, cross one wire over the other, directly below the stem beads. Make sure the beads are tight, then insert the forefinger of one hand in the inverted **V** below

the crossed bare wires. Hold these wires tight. Grasp the beaded strands between the thumb and forefinger of your other hand (your fingers should be about ½" apart). Turn the unit away from you until the wires twist together. This turn will secure the stem beads. Continue to turn the unit until the wires are twisted for about ¼" (Figure 24).

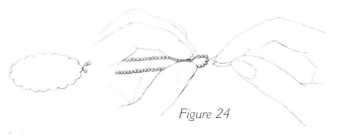

Figure 24

These two beaded wires may be twisted together to make an even more decorative stem. Grasp the unit near the base (where the stem beads begin) in one hand and hold the twisted wires below the stem beads in the other hand. Gently rotate the unit in one direction until the two beaded wires twist together. Take care to avoid twisting too tightly or the beads may chip or break (Figure 25).

Figure 25

If you want to cluster units with two-strand beaded stems, do not twist the wires below the stem beads; use transparent tape instead. The tape will hold the beads in place until you are ready to put the pieces together following the previous instructions for grouping the single beaded stem units.

These smaller stem beaded units are usually bound, singly or in clusters, to a main flower stem. When you want an ambitious creation, you can make bunches of these filler units and fashion them into a spectacular petite bouquet. Simply group the pieces to form several mini clusters (see page 72), but do not taper the bare stem wires. Bundle these units with the twisted wires below the stem beads lined up evenly. Use transparent tape to hold them together temporarily. Wrap these bare wires as if they were one unit with floss, cord, or beaded wire.

Shading, Edging and Tipping

Petals and leaves that are shaded, edged, or tipped with beads of different colors add richness and depth to a flower. The way you do this is fairly simple, but time consuming. However, when you see the results of your efforts, you'll know your time was well spent.

The first step is to decide which construction technique (Basic or Loop) you want to use to make the petal or leaf. Design your pattern next (you can work from memory or follow a sketch), then choose the colors of your beads.

If you are using the Basic Technique and your design calls for shading that begins almost immediately, make the Bottom Basic Loop with unknotted bare spool wire. Then put the Basic Count of beads in your desired colors on the Top Basic Wire. String them one by one, according to the pattern. Knot the end of the Top Basic Wire to keep these beads in place. Estimate the amount of wire you will need to complete the unit by wrapping the bare spool wire loosely around the Basic Count for the required number of rows. Add an extra five or six inches to this measurement and cut the wire from the spool.

Feed the beads for the first row on this open end of wire. String them one by one, according to the pattern, then complete the row. Add beads for the next row in the desired colors, and complete the row. Continue in this manner until you complete the required number of rows. Finish the petal or leaf following the standard Basic Technique procedure.

If you are using different bead colors just to trim the outer edge or the tip of a petal or leaf, you can save a little time by making the solid color rows with beaded spool wire (follow the standard Basic Technique procedure). As you near the end of the unit and are ready to change bead colors, estimate the length of wire needed to complete the piece (don't forget to add the extra inches before you cut the wire from the spool). Finish by stringing the beads, one by one, on the open end of wire according to the pattern and complete the last remaining rows. Finish the petal or leaf following the standard Basic Technique procedure.

It's also possible to design interesting colorations for use with the various Loop Techniques. After you've determined the type, size, and number of loops needed to construct the petal or leaf, simply count and pre-string the beads on the bare spool wire according to the sequence of your pattern.

Make the Loops according to the procedure for the type of Loop you chose. Remember, when you pre-string beads, the last beads on the wire become the first Loop.

If pre-stringing all the beads in sequence seems too complicated, you can string just enough to make one Loop at a time. After you select the type of Loop, measure the length of bare wire you need to complete the unit (multiply the number of Loops times the size of the Loops). Make an allowance for the style of Loop as well (a Crossover Loop needs more wire than a Single Loop). Add an extra 5"–6" for each end (about 12" total) and cut the wire from the spool. Make a knot on one end of the wire. String the beads for the first Loop on the open end of the wire, one by one, according to the pattern. Make the Loop. Add more beads in the desired colors and make another Loop. Move forward along the wire until you complete all Loops needed for the unit. Finish the petal or leaf in the usual manner.

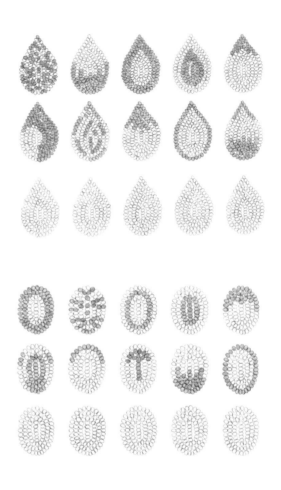

Random Coloring

Very attractive effects can also be achieved with random coloring. In this case, just choose an array of compatible colors and string the beads irregularly on the bare spool wire. Construct the petal or leaf following the normal procedure for whichever technique (Loop or Basic) you use.

Shaping

Shaping plays an important role in the flower making process. It's the finishing touch that adds dimension to the petals and the leaves. It makes the flowers come alive.

Petals and leaves should be shaped before the flower is assembled while you can still take hold of

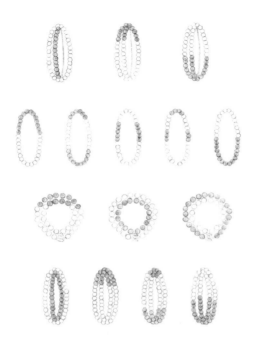

make them less noticeable by gently changing the position of the beads.

Learn to use your hands (fingers, fingertips, knuckles, and palm to cradle the pieces), and the handles of tools, dowels, toothpicks, and other round objects to change shapes for the effects you want to achieve.

Even though this step is left until near the end of the flower-making process, once the pieces are shaped and finally assembled, your flowers burst into bloom, and your efforts are immediately rewarded.

Caring for Your Beaded Flowers

the pieces from every side. You can do some final primping later after putting the flowers together, making minor adjustments to the tips of the flower's petals or the leaves.

Plan to spend some time with shaping. Be flexible and innovative. Variety adds interest. No two flowers ever look exactly alike, and it's not necessary for them to. Some will mimic nature, others can be stylized. You should please yourself—don't always follow the rules.

There are numerous ways to manipulate the pieces to produce the results you want. Cup, curl, or stretch them, and ruffle the edges. Pinch, bend, or press them to sharpen or soften pointed tips. Crease or make them more round; push the beaded rows closer together or spread them slightly apart. Always support the beads. Correct small errors or

Completed beaded flowers need a minimum of care and little maintenance. Flowers used in an arrangement can be dusted with a soft cloth or feather duster as necessary. When the beads need a bit more freshening, spray the flowers with a mild window cleaner or turn them upside down and swish them in a sink filled with mild liquid soap and warm water. Rinse them well, shake and pat them to remove excess water. Hang them upside down outside in hot sun to dry completely or use a hair dryer. You want the flowers to dry quickly to avoid weakening the wire.

For flowers that you have fashioned into jewelry, use a soft cloth dampened with a mild jewelry cleaner. Wipe the beads frequently to maintain their luster. Be sure to gently reshape the petals after every wearing.

Gallery

Columbine, Black-eyed Susan, Blue/Purple Fantasy Flower, Pink/Purple Fantasy Flower, Red/Black Fantasy Flower
Andrea Alyse, Natick, Massachusetts

Lavender
Elaine Cobb, Redwood City, California

Floral Headdresses
Jonalee A. Crabb, Oshkosh, Wisconsin

Blue Iris
Jonalee A. Crabb, Oshkosh, Wisconsin

Nosegay
Linda Havlik,
Newport News, Virginia

Rose, Black Iris, Morning Glory, Daisy
Linda Havlik, Newport News, Virginia

Rose and Iris Pins
Roberta I. Massie, Sandston, Virginia

Daisy Pin
Maryann Patterson-Curtis, Anaheim, California

Iris, Lavender, Daffodil, Asters
Cynthia Peterson, Idaho Springs, Colorado

Hibiscus, Dogwood
Cynthia Peterson, Idaho Springs, Colorado

Daisies
Cynthia Peterson,
Idaho Springs, Colorado

Daisy Pin
Kathy Rees, Orange, California

Nightblooming Cereus,
Kathie Schroeder,
Tucson, Arizona

*Day of the Dead Cross
with Marigolds*
Kathie Schroeder, Tucson, Arizona

Early 1900s Mourning Wreath
from the collection of Linda Havlik

Vintage Garland
from the collection of Kathy Rees

Early 1900s Mourning Wreath
from the collection of the author

Early 1900s Box
from the collection of the author

1880s Wall Pocket
from the collection of the author

1920s Ribbonwork Garland with Beaded Flower Accents
from the collection of the author

1930s Chandelier made in the Victorian Manner
from the collection of Marvin Alexander, Inc., New York, New York

Projects

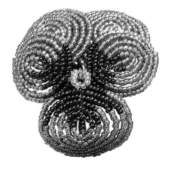

Clover Pin

FOR GREAT RESULTS, make this natural-looking floral pin using the Continuous Single Loop Technique.

Materials

Size 11° seed beads:
    One hank pink or plum for flowers and bud
    One hank moss green for leaves and calyx
    One spool 28-gauge gold or silver beading wire
    One spool 34-gauge gold or silver beading wire
1" pin clasp with prongs
One skein green embroidery floss or stranded silk
Water-soluble white glue
½ yard ¼" moss green ribbon

Notions

Wire cutters
Needle-nose pliers with smooth jaws
Ruler
Wire straighteners
Scissors
Wire spool holders
Toothpicks

Flower Petals

Make two.

Using 28-gauge wire and plum beads, make Continuous Single Loops, five on one wire, ¾" beads per Loop.

Make two.

Using 28-gauge wire and plum beads, make Continuous Single Loops, eight on one wire, 1" beads per Loop.

Flower Calyx

Make two.

Using 28-gauge wire and green beads, make Continuous Single Loops, five on one wire with one bead between each Loop, ⅝" beads per Loop. The extra bead between the Loops enlarges the center opening in the calyx to accommodate the stem wire extensions below the petals. Be sure to count the number of beads that make ⅝" before you make the first Loop.

Slide one bead from the beaded spool wire close to the base of the first Loop. Count the number of beads needed for the second Loop and make it next to the extra bead with Wire B.

Slide one bead from the beaded spool wire close to the base of the second Loop. Count the number of beads needed for the third Loop and make it next to the extra bead with Wire B. Repeat the process to make the fourth and fifth Loops.

Slide one bead from the beaded spool wire close to the fifth Loop to complete the sequence (this bead will be between the fifth and first Loop) and finish the unit. See Figure 1.

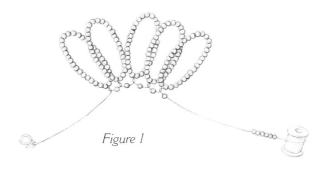

Figure 1

Bud Petals

Make one.

Using 28-gauge wire and green beads, make Continuous Single Loops, five on one wire, ¾" beads per Loop.

Bud Calyx

Make one.

Using 28-gauge wire and green beads, make Continuous Single Loops, three on one wire, with one bead between each Loop, ⅝" beads per Loop. Make the bud calyx the same way you made the flower calyx.

Leaves

Make four.

Using 28-gauge wire and green beads, make Continuous Single Loops, four on one wire, 1" beads per Loop. Pinch sides together to narrow the Loops as you make them. Finish the unit as instructed in Continuous Single Loops (page 27), but flatten the Loops instead of leaving them bunched together (they should stand up like the four fingers of your hand).

Flower Assembly

Assemble the flower by stacking one 5-Loop petal and one 8-Loop petal. Then insert the stem wires below these petals down into the center of one 5-Loop calyx unit.

Thread the stem wire extensions below one 5-Loop petal through the middle of one 8-Loop petal. Push them together so the small petal is nestled within the large petal.

Straighten the stem wires and trim the ends evenly. Push these wires through the opening in the center of one 5-Loop calyx unit. Pull the stem wires down and simultaneously push the calyx up against the bottom of the clover. See Figure 2.

Repeat the process to assemble the remaining flower.

Figure 2

Bud Assembly

Thread the stem wire extensions below the bud down into the center of the 3-Loop calyx unit the same way as the flower.

Stem Wrapping

Use 3 strands of embroidery floss (six-ply is too thick for the delicate stems) or stranded silk for the final finish on all the stems. Wrap each stem for the entire length desired according to the directions provided in Stem Coverings.

Finishing

Group the flowers, bud, and leaves to make a small bouquet. Use a clothespin or piece of transparent tape to hold the stems together temporarily. Cut a 10" length of bare 34-gauge wire. Leave a 2" wire extension and put the rest of the wire against the stems slightly below the clustered flowers. Hold the wire and the stems between the thumb and forefinger of one hand and use your other hand to wrap the longer end

Figure 3

of the 34-gauge wire in a tight spiral around the entire bouquet (Figure 3).

Remove the clothespin or tape.

Keep the wraps close together. Do not wind straight down the stems.

When the stems are securely bound together, wrap back to the starting point and the 2" wire extension. Cross one wire over the other and twist them together for about ¼". Trim away the remaining untwisted wires close to the last twist. Use the tip of your needle-nose pliers to smooth the cut

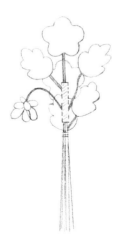

Figure 4

ends and press the twisted wires next to the stems.

Cut a 4" length of the same floss used to wrap the stems. Use a toothpick to dab a little glue on the binding wires. Starting from the back side of the bouquet, press one end of the floss against the binding wires and into the glue. Take the other end of the floss and wrap it around the binding wires to cover them. Keep the thread smooth and flat as you wind.

End the wrapping on the back side of the bouquet. Trim the floss and dab a bit more glue on the thread ends. Use your fingers to smooth them against the covered binding wires. Allow the glue to dry.

Position the pin clasp on the back side of the bouquet with the catch pointing down the stem (the pin should be closer to the top of the bouquet than near the middle to keep the pin from falling forward when you wear it). Slip the prongs over several flower stems. Use the tip of your needle-nose pliers to bend the prongs around the stems. Pinch them closed to keep the pin securely in place (Figure 4).

Tie a bow around the stem just below the clustered flowers. Trim both ends of the ribbon on the diagonal.

Curl the tips of the petals and bend the leaves. Rearrange flowers as necessary.

Rose Pin

MAKE THIS BEAUTIFUL ROSE PIN to liven up the lapel of a coat or suit.

Materials

Size 11° seed beads:
    One hank rose for petals
    One hank green for leaves and calyx (sepals)
    One spool 26-gauge gold or silver beading wire
    One spool 34-gauge gold or silver beading wire
1¼" pin clasp
One skein embroidery floss, cotton, or stranded
    silk, or 5 yards nylon cording
Water-soluble white glue

Notions

Wire cutters
Needle-nose pliers with smooth jaws
Ruler
Wire straighteners
Scissors
Wire spool holders
Toothpicks
Pen or similar round object

Petals

Make two.

Using 26-gauge wire and rose seed beads, make a ½" Basic, Rows 7, Round Top, Round Bottom. Leave 10" bare wire for Bottom Basic Loop. Cut open the Bottom Basic Loop to make two stem wire extensions.

Make five.

Using 26-gauge wire and rose seed beads, make a ½" Basic, Rows 9, Round Top, Round Bottom, Reverse Wrap on Bottom. Leave 10" bare wire for Bottom Basic Loop. Cut open the Bottom Basic Loop to make two stem wire extensions.

Center

Make one.

Using 26-gauge wire and rose seed beads, make 1½" Basic, Rows 3, Round Top, Round Bottom. Spiral the Center around a pen or similar round object. Tuck the tip down into the spiral to hide the trimmed end of the Top Basic Wire (Figure 1). Cut open the Bottom Basic Loop to make two stem wire extensions.

Figure 1

Sepals

Make four.

Using 26-gauge wire and green seed beads, make ½" Basic, Rows 5, Pointed Top, Round Bottom, Reverse Wrap on Bottom. Leave 10" bare wire for Bottom Basic Loop. Cut open the Bottom Basic Loop to make two stem wire extensions.

Leaves

Make two.

Using 26-gauge wire and green seed beads, make ½" Basic, Rows 5, Pointed Top, Round Bottom.

Leave 10" bare wire for Bottom Basic Loop. Cut open the Bottom Basic Loop to make two stem wire extensions.

Make one.

Using 26-gauge wire and green seed beads, make ½" Basic, Rows 7, Pointed Top, Round Bottom. Leave 10" bare wire for Bottom Basic Loop. Cut open the Bottom Basic Loop to make two stem wire extensions.

Shaping

Shape the petals and leaves before assembling them. Curve the sides of the two 7-Row petals over a pen, your pinkie finger, or a similar round object (make them look like a fingernail). The wrong side (where the wire shows) should be on the inside of the curve (Figure 2).

Figure 2

Cup the bottoms of the five 9-Row petals. Put them in the palm of your hand, one by one, with the wrong side (where the Reverse Wrapped wire shows on the bottom) facing you. Use the handle of your pliers or your thumb and push firmly against the beads. Use your fingers to roll the tips of these petals outward or arch them by curving them over a round object (like a pen). Bend each petal sharply down at the base (Figure 3).

Shape the four sepals the same way. Bend and curve the leaves as desired.

Reduce the wires below the

Figure 3

two 7-Row petals. Reduce the wires below any three of the five 9-Row petals.

Rose and Sepal Assembly

The rose is assembled by binding the petals and sepals together. First straighten all stem wire extensions. Fasten the 34-gauge wire to the spiraled center according to the directions in the Flower Assembly Section (page 62). Put the two 7-Row petals on opposite sides of the center with the wrong sides facing in (the side where the wire shows). Wrap the assembly wire around the bottom of these petals twice, tightly. The center should be nestled snugly between the two side petals (Figure 4).

Figure 4

Bind on the five remaining petals, one at a time, spacing them evenly around the center unit (Figure 5).

Make sure you place the wrong side of each petal (where the wire

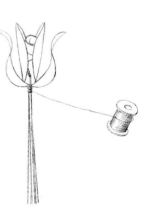

Figure 5

shows at the bottom) against the right side of the petals that you have already bound to the stem.

Wrap the assembly wire tightly and do not allow the petals to slip down the stem (keep them close to the bottom of the flower).

Add the sepals one by one, placing the wrong side of the sepal (where the wire shows at the bottom) against the right side of the flower petals. Space the sepals evenly and keep them close to the bottom of the flower. Do not let them slip down the stem.

Once you have bound these parts together, bring the wire to the bottom of the stem as instructed in Flower Assembly.

Stem Covering

The main stem of the rose requires a preliminary wrap with floss to provide a color background for the final stem finish. Apply this floss foundation to the main stem according to the directions provided in Stem Coverings (page 66).

I used embroidery floss for the final finish on the stems of the leaves. Straighten the stem wires. Cut a 12" length of floss for each leaf. Wrap the stems of the two small leaves for ½" according to the directions provided in Stem Coverings. Leave the wires below the floss covering bare.

Use the same procedure to wrap the stem of the large leaf for ¾". Leave the wires below the floss covering bare.

Finishing

I also used embroidery floss for the final finish on the main flower stem. Begin the final floss wrap according to the directions provided in Stem Coverings (page 66). Wrap the floss for approximately ¼". Stop and glue the pin clasp in position on the back side of the stem. (The pin opens easier if you place the catch down the stem.) Allow the glue to dry.

Continue with the floss wrapping, covering the stem and the pin bar at the same time. Use the floss to bind on the leaves as you come to their position (cluster them or stagger them unevenly), at the same time covering the main stem and the stem wires left bare below the leaves. Continue wrapping the floss to the stem length desired. Finish as instructed in Stem Coverings (page 66).

Gently adjust the petals and leaves. Bend the full bloom slightly forward.

Pansy Pin

PANSIES WERE AMONG the most popular flowers of the 1800s. The name "pansy" comes from the French, *pensez à moi,* which means "think of me."

Pansies don't need to be shy flowers. Bow their necks, but turn their faces up. Arch the bud's stem to make it sway gracefully. Do the same with the leaf.

Materials

Size 11° seed beads:

One hank lavender for flower petals and bud
Partial hank black for flower petal contrast
Partial hank yellow for flower center and stamen
One hank forest green for leaf and calyx
One spool 26-gauge gold or silver beading wire
One spool 28-gauge gold or silver beading wire
One spool 34-gauge gold or silver beading wire
1¼" pin clasp
Five yards Conso® #18 bonded nylon thread
Water-soluble white glue

Notions

Wire cutters
Needle-nose pliers with smooth jaws
Ruler
Wire straighteners
Scissors
Wire spool holders
Toothpicks

Bud

Make one.

Using 28-gauge wire, make Continuous Single Loops, four on one wire, 1¼" beads per Loop. Pinch sides together to narrow the Loops as you make them. Pull the stem wires up above the Loops.

Calyx

Make two—one for the bud, the other for the pansy.

Using 28-gauge wire, make Continuous Single Loops, five on one wire, ⅝" beads per Loop (Figure 1).

Figure 1

Turn the work so that Wire A and Loop #1 (the first Loop made) are on the right and Wire B and Loop #5 (the last Loop made) are on the left.

Slide beads from the spool toward Loop #5. Form a Single Loop with 1¼" of beads below Loop #5. Do not twist the Loop to secure it. Push the remaining beads back toward the spool. Make sure the beads in the Loop are tight. Bring bare Wire B over the wire between Loop #5 and Loop #4 and bend it sharply down so it rests on top of the wire between these two Loops (Figure 2).

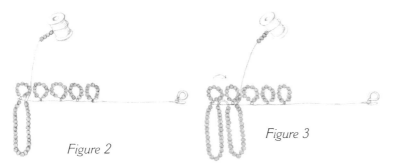

Figure 2

Figure 3

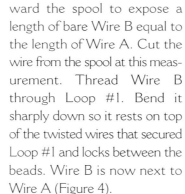

Figure 4

Form a Single Loop with 1¼" of beads below Loop #4. Bring bare Wire B over the wire between Loop #4 and Loop #3. Bend it sharply down so it rests on top of the wire between these two Loops (Figure 3).

Repeat this process below Loop #3 and Loop #2. Form the last Single Loop with 1¼" of beads below Loop #1. Slide the remaining beads back toward the spool to expose a length of bare Wire B equal to the length of Wire A. Cut the wire from the spool at this measurement. Thread Wire B through Loop #1. Bend it sharply down so it rests on top of the twisted wires that secured Loop #1 and locks between the beads. Wire B is now next to Wire A (Figure 4).

Cross Wire B over Wire A close to the beads. Hold the Loop unit with one hand. Insert the forefinger of your other hand in the inverted **V** below the crossed wires. Hold these wires tight and use your finger to push them against the beads. Turn the Loop unit away from you to twist the two wires together two times.

Thread the end of bare Wire B through Loop #5. Pull the wire to close the calyx circle, bringing Wire B back to Wire A. Cross Wire B over Wire A and twist the two wires together two times as before.

Straighten both wires. Trim the ends evenly, cutting away the wire knot. These wires become part of the stem. Pull the stem wires up toward the ⅝" Loops for the pansy bud. Pull the stem wires down toward the 1¼" Loops for the pansy.

Center
Make one.

Using 26-gauge wire, make one Single Loop using ⅝" of beads. Twist the wire below the Loop for ¼". Bend the Loop forward at the base so it resembles an upside down ladle.

Stamen
Make one.

Using 34-gauge wire, thread one yellow bead on 10" of wire cut from the spool. Slide the bead to the middle and fold the wire in half. Cross one wire over the other directly below the bead. Twist both wires together tightly for 1". (Turn the bead instead of the bare wires for a neater twist.) Straighten both wires, trimming the ends evenly. These wires become part of the stem.

Pansy Back Petals
Make two.

Using 26-gauge wire and lavender beads, make a Basic 3, Rows 13, Round Top, Round Bottom. Leave 10" of bare wire for the Bottom Basic Loop.

Finish the unit as in a Round Basic except wrap the bare spool wire five times tightly around the Bottom Basic Loop instead of twice. Cut open the Bottom Basic Loop to make two stem wire extensions.

Pansy Side Petals

Make two.

Using 26-gauge wire and lavender and black beads, make a Basic 3, Rows 11, Round Top, Round Bottom. Leave 10" of bare wire for the Bottom Basic Loop.

To make a "face" on the pansy, string beads on the Basic one by one according to the design of your choice. Refer to the instructions in the Shading, Edging, and Tipping section (page 74), beginning with a Basic as directed. Allow 24" of bare wire to complete the petal and cut this measurement from the spool. Wrap around the Basic Count in the normal manner, right to left, adding beads following your pattern. Count and note the number of beads per color in each Row as you complete them. This sequence will be duplicated for the other side petal, making a mirror image that will match when the pansy is assembled. Finish the unit the same way as the pansy back petals.

To make a second side petal, follow the same procedure except wrap around the Basic Count left to right instead of right to left. Use the same number of beads per color in each Row. By changing the direction of the wraps and using the same number of beads and colors, you will make the left side of one petal match the right side of the other.

Pansy Bottom Petal

Make one.

Using 26-gauge wire, make a Basic 3, Rows 13, Round Top, Round Bottom. Leave 10" bare wire for the Bottom Basic Loop.

Complete the pansy's face in the same manner as the side petals by stringing beads on the Basic, one by one, according to the pattern. Because you're making just one unit, it's not necessary to note the number of beads per color in each Row and you can wrap the Rows around the Basic Count in the normal manner. Be sure to begin your design at the Bottom Basic Loop because the base of the petal will be near the center when the pansy is assembled (the top of the petal points down). Finish the unit the same way you did the pansy back petals.

Leaf

Make one.

Using 26-gauge wire and green beads, make a Loopback Basic 14, Rows 7, Round Top, Round Bottom. Leave 10" bare wire for the Bottom Basic Loop. Make the Loopbacks as follows: #1—2⅛" beads; #2— 2⅝" beads; #3—2⅛" beads; #4—1½" beads.

Finish the leaf as in Round Basics except wrap the bare spool wire three times tightly around the Bottom Basic Loop instead of two times and do not trim the spool wire close to the last wrap. Instead, bring this bare wire down toward the bottom of the Bottom Basic Loop to reinforce the leaf stem.

Cut open the Bottom Basic Loop to make two stem wire extensions. Cut the spool wire close to these wires, trimming the three ends evenly. Straighten the stem wire extensions below the leaf.

Shaping

Shape the pansy petals and leaf before they are assembled. Gently cup the two back petals by pushing the beads forward from the wrong side (where the wire shows). This should make the petals look like a shallow bowl.

Repeat the process to cup each side petal, then put each petal between the thumb and index finger of one hand (hold it at the top and bottom of the petal). Press down gently to compress the beads and make a slight oval.

Shape the pansy bottom petal the same as the side petals except press down firmly to spread the rows into a horizontal oval and make the cupping more pronounced. Bend the petal forward at the base.

Arch and bend the Basic center of the leaf. Curve the Loopbacks, bending two up and two down to make them look natural.

Pansy Assembly

Assemble the pansy by inserting the stem wires below the petals, center, and stamen down into the center opening in a calyx unit in the following order: two back petals, two side petals, center, and stamen (put the stamen in the middle of the center), and bottom petal.

The small Loops of the calyx rest against the petals and the large Loops point down the stem. Pull the stem wires down and simultaneously push the calyx up against the back side of the pansy.

Bud Assembly

Thread the stem wires of the bud up through the center opening in the other calyx unit. The large Loops should cradle the bud and the small Loops should be on top like a crown.

Stem Covering

Use nylon cording for the final finish on all the stems.

Wrap the stem of the leaf for ½" to ¾" (or longer, if desired) according to the directions provided in the Stem Coverings section (page 66). Use the same procedure to wrap the stem of the bud for 1 ⅝" to 1¾".

Follow the same directions to begin the cord wrap on the main stem of the pansy and wrap for approximately ½". Stop and glue the pin clasp in position on the back side of the stem. Place the catch down the stem. Allow the glue to dry.

Continue with the cord wrapping, covering the stem and the pin bar at the same time. Use the cord to bind on the bud and the leaf as you come to their positions, covering the main stem and the bare stem wires of these units simultaneously.

Wrap for ¼", stop and taper three or four main stem wires to lessen the bulk added by the bud and leaf stem wires. Continue wrapping the cord to the stem length desired. Finish as instructed in the Stem Coverings section.

Sunflower Pin

BRING A RAY OF SUNSHINE into your life by working up this beautiful sunflower.

Materials

Size 10° seed beads:
    One hank orange for flower petals
    Partial hank brown for flower center
    Partial hank green mix for leaves
One spool 26-gauge gold or silver beading wire
One spool 34-gauge gold or silver beading wire
1" pin clasp with two holes
⅞" flat gold or silver filigree disk
Transparent tape

Notions

Wire cutters
Needle-nose pliers with smooth jaws
Ruler
Wire straighteners
Wire spool holders
Pen or similar round object

Petals

Make seven.

Using 26-gauge wire and orange seed beads, make a Basic 5, Rows 7, Pointed Top, Round Bottom. Leave 8" bare wire for Bottom Basic Loop. Cut open Bottom Basic Loop to make two stem wire extensions.

Leaves

Make three.

Using 26-gauge wire and green seed beads, make a Basic 4, Rows 9, Pointed Top, Round Bottom. Shade with two colors. Leave 10" bare wire for Bottom Basic Loop. Cut open Bottom Basic Loop to make two stem wire extensions.

Bring both wire extensions together to form a single stem and stem bead (page 72) each unit. Use the same size seed bead as the leaf and match or contrast the color as desired. (If the beads do not fit on both wires easily, reduce one wire from each unit.)

Vary the length of each beaded stem between 2" and 3" and leave the wire that remains below the beads (about 1") bare. Put a small piece of tape around the bare wire to hold the stem beads in place temporarily.

Wrap the beaded stems around a pen or similar round object to coil them loosely.

Center

Make one.

Using 26-gauge wire and brown seed beads, make a Flat Disk Basic 1, Rows 10–12, Round Top, Round Bottom. Leave 10" bare wire for Bottom Basic Loop.

Construct the center after you mount the petals and leaves on the wire support. The unit should be made large enough to cover the opening in the middle of the flower (it usually takes between 10 to 12 Rows).

If the required number of Rows is even, finish the center as in Dome Basics, with a pair of wire extensions at both ends.

If the required number of Rows is uneven, finish the center as in Round Basics except leave the Top Basic Wire long, trimming away only the wire knot. The center will have only one wire extension at one end (Top Basic Wire) and two wire extensions at the other end (Bottom Basic Loop cut open), instead of the usual pair at both ends.

Wire Support

Make one.

Cut a 7" length of bare 26-gauge wire. Make a ⅞" diameter double circle with this wire. (You can curve the wire twice around a nickel—it's the perfect size.) Use a small piece of tape to hold the cut ends of the wire in place temporarily (Figure 1).

Figure 1

Assembly

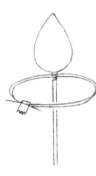

Mount petals and leaves on the wire support one at a time. Pick up one petal, right side facing you. Put both stem wire extensions inside the wire circle (Figure 2).

Rest the bottom of the petal on the top edge of the circle. Hold the petal in place with one hand and use the other hand to wind the stem

Figure 2

wire extension at the right of the petal tightly around the wire circle. Bring the extension under the wire circle, loop it over, around, and back down into the circle again. Wind it side by side, not over itself, four or five times (Figure 3).

Keep the wraps close (push them together with your thumbnail). End the last wrap inside the circle. Trim the wire close and use the tip of your needle-nose pliers to smooth the cut end of the wire.

Still holding the petal, wind the stem wire extension at the left of the petal tightly around the wire circle and finish it the same way (Figure 4).

Pick up another petal and repeat the process. Space the petals evenly as you fill the entire circle (the petals will overlap slightly at their widest part).

Remove the tape when you come to it. Make sure to incorporate the ends of the wire support into the circle by winding the stem wire extensions over them.

Use the same procedure to mount the leaves on the wire support as you come to their position. The beaded stems should appear to be underneath the flower petals.

If you reduced the pair of wire extensions to one in order to Stem Bead, the wire that remains can be wound around the circle to the right or to the left.

Make sure the beads are close together on the stem to avoid bare wire showing between them.

Continue in this manner until you have mounted all the petals and leaves.

Put the center on top of the flower and press it down firmly.

Figure 3

Figure 4

If the unit has an even number of rows, place one pair of bare wire extensions over the outside edge of the wire support between two petals on one side of the flower. Place the other pair of extensions over the outside edge of the wire support between two petals on the opposite side. If the unit has an odd number of Rows, you'll have one pair of wire extensions on one side and just the Top Basic Wire on the other side. However, the center is still attached to the flower in the same manner.

Bend these wires so they meet in the middle on the underside of the flower. Use your fingers to press them close to the wire support where they curve over the edge.

Twist the wires together three times to secure the center to the flower. Trim away the remaining untwisted wires close to the last twist. Press the twisted part flat against the underside of the center.

Attach the pin clasp to the filigree disk with wire. Cut a 14" length of bare 34-gauge wire. Pick up the filigree with the right side facing you. Take one end of the wire and push it from the back to the front through an opening in the design (choose a section near where the pin clasp will be) (Figure 5).

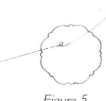

Figure 5

Leave a 2" length of wire on the back side of the filigree. Loop the wire over part of the filigree and push it to the back again. Bring the wire to the front through the same opening you used the first time and pull the wire tight to anchor it.

Thread the wire through one of the holes in the pin clasp. Push the pin clasp against the filigree. To keep the sunflower from falling forward when you wear it, position the pin clasp in the upper third of the filigree (Figure 6).

Figure 6

Loop the wire over the pin clasp, push it down into an opening in the filigree and bring it back up through the same hole in the pin clasp. Pull the wire tight. Repeat this process several times.

Move the wire to the other hole in the pin clasp (bring it up from the back to the front). Loop the wire over the pin clasp, then thread it in and out of this hole in the same way.

When the pin clasp is securely fastened, push the wire to the back of the filigree to meet the 2" end left at the starting point. Twist these wires together three times.

Trim away the remaining untwisted wires close to the last twist. Press the twisted part flat against the filigree disk (Figure 7).

Figure 7

Attach the filigree disk to the flower with wire. Cut a 20" length of bare 34-gauge wire. Pick up the filigree with the pin clasp facing you. Take one end of the wire and thread it from the back to the front through an opening in the design near the edge.

Leave a 2" length of wire extension, then loop the long end of the wire over the edge and bring it to the front again. Pull the wire tight to anchor it. Put the filigree on top of the wire support on the back of the flower. (It's a good idea to position the filigree so the two leaves and their weight are below the pin clasp.)

Hold the filigree in place with one hand and use the other hand to loop the wire over the edge of the filigree (thread it through the design openings), and wrap it around the wire support at the same time (Figure 8).

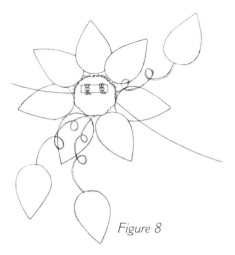

Figure 8

Pull the wire tight as you work around the filigree and the wire support, back to the starting point and the 2" wire end. Twist these wires together three times, next to the edge of the filigree. Trim away the remaining untwisted wires close to the last twist. Use the tip of your needle-nose pliers to gently curve the twisted wires under the filigree disk.

Shaping

Curve the tip of each petal down slightly. Bend the base of two or three petals up to add dimension to the flower. Cup and curve the leaves. Adjust the coiled stems, pulling them away from the flower so they dangle delicately beneath the petals.

Chrysanthemum with Lacy Fern Pin

THIS PROJECT EVOKES a Victorian look with its sumptuous use of beads.

Materials

Size 11° round or two-cut or size 9° three-cut seed beads:

Two hanks pink/lavender/blue mix for flower petals

One hank deep green for fern sprigs

Two spools 34-gauge silver beading wire

One 12" piece 16- or 18-gauge straight-cut wire

1½" pin clasp

Silver glass glitter

One bundle store-bought flower stamens

One skein embroidery floss or stranded silk or five yards nylon cording

Water-soluble white glue

Notions

Wire cutters

Needle-nose pliers with smooth jaws

Ruler

Wire straighteners

Scissors

Wire spool holders

Toothpicks

Petals

Make twenty-five.

Measure and cut a 35" length of bare 34-gauge wire. String on one pink bead and slide it 10" from one end of the wire. Hold the bead in place with one hand and use the other hand to loop the end of the wire over, around, and through the bead again (Figure 1).

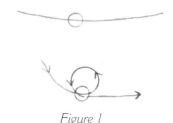

Figure 1

Pull the wire tight to anchor the bead at this measurement (the wire should curve closely around the outside of the bead).

String 10", 11", or 12" of pink, lavender, and blue beads on the long end of the wire (to shade the petal, string one color for about 2" or 3", then another color and so on, until the required measurement of beads has been strung). Knot the end of the wire to keep the beads from sliding off. Fold the wire where the single bead is anchored. Put the 10"

Vintage flower from the collection of Kathy Gastellu. Torrance, California

end next to the piece of 12" straight cut wire. Use the thumb and forefinger of one hand to hold this wire and the straight-cut together directly below the single bead (Figure 2).

Take the long end of the wire in your other hand and let the beads slide down to the single bead.

Begin the coil close to the single bead by wrapping the beaded wire around the straight-cut and the 10" length of wire simultaneously (Figure 3).

Keep the rows close together. Leave a little slack between the beads to keep them from breaking as you wrap the coils. Continue winding in this manner until you've used all the strung beads.

Do not remove the straight-cut wire from the beaded coil. Hold the last strung bead in place with your fingers and secure the coil by winding the bare wire below the last bead for ¼". Wrap the wire side by side, not over itself. Push the wraps close to the last bead with your fingernail.

Roll the beaded coils between your fingers to round and make them more even. Stretch the coils slightly. Carefully remove the straight-cut wire from the petal.

Straighten the bare wires that remain below the beads (these end wires become part of the flower stem). Trim the ends evenly, cutting away the wire knot (Figure 4).

Figure 2

Figure 3

Stamen Bundle

Make one.

Open the bundle of stamens by untwisting the wire that holds them together. Take out as many as you need for the flower center, then re-wrap the wire around the stamens you're not using.

Pour a little glitter in a disposable shallow dish. (Caution: Do not rub your eyes or put your hands to your face when working with the glass glitter.) Dip the ends of the stamen, one by one, in white glue thinned to the consistency of heavy cream. Do not use too much glue or the stamen ends will be too big.

Roll the glue-dipped ends in the glass glitter. Put the stamens on a paper towel or napkin and allow them to dry thoroughly.

Make a bundle of the glittery stamens. Cut a 16" length of 34-gauge wire. Fold the wire in half around the middle of the stamen bundle. Fold the stamens in half (pull all the ends straight up) and twist the wire tightly for about 1". You can make the twists tighter if you turn the stamen bundle instead of the bare wires (Figure 5).

Figure 4

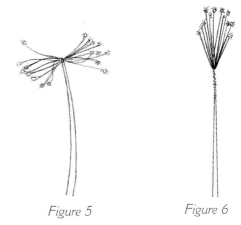

Figure 5   *Figure 6*

The stamen bundle should stand straight up on the wire. Straighten the wires (they become part of the flower stem) and trim both ends evenly (Figure 6).

Lacy Fern

Make five.

Using 34-gauge wire make Continuous Single Loops, five or six beads per Loop.

Make Loops in varying numbers (7–17) to form leaves. Twist bare wires below Loops to form twig stems. Twist bare wires below twigs to form main stem.

Twisted twig and main stem wires are left bare (no additional stem covering is required).

String 10" of beads on the spool wire. Make the first Single Loop 10" from the knotted end of the wire (Wire A) as instructed in Single Loops. Continue twisting the wires (Wire A and Wire B) together neatly underneath the Loop for ½" (Figure 7).

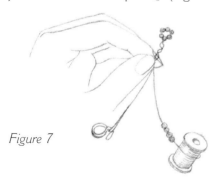

Figure 7

You can make the twists smooth and tight if you turn the Loop instead of the bare wires. Hold the two wires parallel and grip them between the thumb and forefinger of one hand and turn the Loop with the other hand. Twist down the wires. The twisted

½" length of wire below the first Loop is the first stem of the twig.

Leave ½" of Wire B bare and make a second Single Loop. Twist the wires underneath this Loop (you are twisting two bare portions of Wire B) back to the twisted wire twig stem below the first Loop (Figure 8).

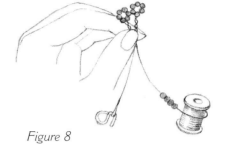

Figure 8

Leave ½" of Wire B bare and make a third Single Loop. Twist the wires underneath this Loop (you are twisting two bare portions of Wire B) back to where the two twisted wire twig stems meet.

Cross bare Wire B over bare Wire A directly below where the three twisted twig stems meet. Twist these two wires together for ½" (you are twisting the knotted end and the spool end of the wire). These twisted wires form the main stem (Figure 9).

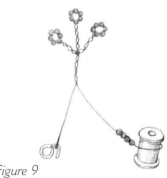

Figure 9

The length of the bare wire extensions determines the length of the twig stems. If you want a shorter twig stem, leave a ¼" extension; for a longer twig stem, leave ¾" to 1".

The fern spray looks more delicate and natural when you vary the length of the twig stems. Leave ¾" of Wire B bare and make a fourth Single Loop. Twist the wires underneath this Loop (you are twisting two bare portions of Wire B) back to the twisted wire main stem.

Leave ¾" of Wire B bare and make a fifth Single Loop. Twist the wires underneath this Loop (you are twisting two bare portions of Wire B) back to the twisted wire twig stem below the fourth Loop.

Cross bare Wire B over bare Wire A directly below where the twisted twig stems of the fourth and fifth Loops meet. Twist these two wires together for ½" (you are twisting the knotted end and the spool end of the wire). These twisted wires add length to the main stem.

Make another pair of Loops exactly the same way. Bend them to the left of the main stem. Cross bare Wire B over bare Wire A and twist them together as before to add another ½" length to the main stem (Figure 10).

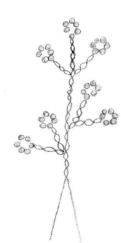

Figure 10

To make a branch extension off the main stem, leave 1" of Wire B bare. Make a Single Loop. Twist the wires underneath this Loop for ½", not back to the twisted wire main stem. (There is still ½" of bare wire remaining from the original inch.)

Leave ½" of Wire B bare and make another Loop. Twist the wires underneath this Loop back to the twisted wire twig stem below the first Loop on the branch.

Leave ½" of Wire B bare and make another Loop. Twist the wires underneath this Loop all the way back to the main stem. This completes the branch (Figure 11).

Cross bare Wire B over bare Wire A and twist them together as before to add length to the main stem. Continue in this manner, making Loops in irregular numbers (on

Figure 11

twisted wire twig stems and branches) and adding length to the main stem, as desired.

To finish one Fern unit, twist the main stem wires (Wire A and Wire B) together 1" beyond the last twig or branch. Leave a length of bare Wire B equal to the remaining untwisted length of Wire A and cut the wire from the spool at this measurement (don't forget to knot the end of the spool Wire B to prevent any strung beads from sliding off).

Straighten these bare wires (they become part of the flower stem). Trim the ends evenly, cutting away the wire knot (Figure 12).

Figure 12

Assembly

Assemble the chrysanthemum by binding the petals, stamen bundle, and fern together. Unwind about 10" of 34-gauge wire, but do not cut it from the spool. Take the end of the wire and push 2" through the stamen bundle. Bend this 2" end down the stem.

Wrap the wire three times tightly around the stamen bundle and over itself at the same time. This wrapping holds the stamen stalks together and secures the wire to the stem.

Bind the petals to the stem one at a time, at first spacing them evenly around the stamen bundle and then as precisely as possible at openings between the petals already bound to the stem.

Keep the assembly wire close to the base of the flower, wrapping it tightly over itself each time. Bend each petal down at its base before placing it in position to keep the bottom of the flower flat. Do not let these petals slip down the stem.

Put the last six petals around the flower wherever they look the most attractive (they can be bound a little lower on the stem, if necessary). Add the ferns close to the bottom of the flower. Space them evenly around it or clustered to one side.

Wrap the assembly wire around the fern stems just below the twisted wires.

Once you have bound these parts together, bring the wire to the bottom of the stem as instructed in Flower Assembly (page 62).

Stem Covering

The main stem of the Chrysanthemum requires a preliminary wrap with floss to provide a background of color for the final stem finish. Apply this floss foundation to the main stem according to the directions provided in Stem Coverings (page 66).

Finishing

Embroidery floss, silk, or nylon cording may be used for the final finish on the main flower stem. Begin the final floss or cord wrap as directed in Stem Coverings (page 66).

Wrap the floss or cord for about $\frac{3}{8}$". Stop and glue the pin clasp in position on the back side of the stem. (The pin opens easier if you place the catch down the stem.) Allow the glue to dry.

Continue with the wrapping, covering the stem and the pin bar at the same time.

Wrap the floss or cord to the stem length desired. Because this flower is heavy, a short 2" to 2 $\frac{1}{4}$" stem is best.

Finish as instructed in Stem Coverings (page 66).

Shaping

Curve the tips of the petals toward the center of the flower. Bend and curve the fern twigs and the branches, rearranging them as necessary to look feathery and airy.

Bibliography/Sources

Crabb, Jonalee A. *The Origins of French Beaded Flowers*. Oshkosh, Wisconsin: Independent research paper, 2000.

Kling, Candace. *The Artful Ribbon*. Lafayette, California: C & T Publishing, 1996.

Schroeder, Kathie. "Des Fleurs en Fil et Perles: A French Tradition." *Beadwork,* Winter 1999.

Sources

Arlene Baker
7470 Lubec St.
Downey, CA 90240
(562) 928-3583
(562) 928-3583 fax
Classes available.

Caravan Beads
449 Forest Ave.
Portland, ME 04101
(800) 230-8941
(207) 874-2664 fax
www.caravanbeads.com

Creative Castle
2321 Michael Dr.
Newbury Park, CA 91320
(805) 499-1377
www.creativecastle.com
Beads. Classes available.

Eastern Findings Corp.
19 W. 34th St.
New York, NY 10001
(800) EFC-6640
(212) 629-4018 fax
www.efcsales@easternfindings.com

Fire Mountain Gems
One Fire Mountain Wy.
Grants Pass, OR 97526-2373
(800) 355-2137
www.questions@firemtn.com

Garden of Beadin'
PO Box 1535
Redway, CA 95560
(800) 232-3588
www.gardenofbeadin.com

General Bead
637 Minna St.
San Francisco, CA 94103
(415) 621-8187
www.genbead.com

Linda Havlik
2 Garland Dr.
Newport News, VA 23606
(757) 599-6346
www.beadedflowersinc@cs.com
Silk threads.

Ornamental Resources
PO Box 3010
Idaho Springs, CO 80452
(800) 876-6762
Beads.www.ornabead.com

Piecemakers
1720 Adams Ave.
Costa Mesa, CA 92626
(714) 641-3112
(714) 641-2883 fax
www.piecemakers.com
Beads. Classes available.

Shipwreck Beads
2500 Mottman Rd. SW
Olympia, WA 98512
(800) 950-4232
www.shipwreck-beads.com

The San Gabriel Bead Company
8970 Huntington Dr.
San Gabriel, CA 91775
(626) 614-0014
(626) 614-0173 fax
www.beadcompany.com
Classes available.

Stone Mountain Colorado
PO Box 1250
110 East 7th St.
Walsenburg, CO 81089
(888) 423-2370
Vintage beads.

Yodamo, Inc.
2023 East Sims Wy., Ste. 183
Port Townsend, WA 98368
(360) 379-3250
(360) 379-2839 fax
www.eternasilk.com
Silk threads.

Index

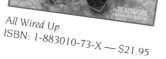

Vintage flower. Collection of the author.